Welcome to *Facts That'll Blow Your Mind!*

Hey there, curious thinker!
You just opened a book packed with the weid most
amazing facts ever. Inside, you'll find stories
— but they are! From glowing jellyfish and
dollar mistakes and viral internet legends, e
want to tell your friends about.
This isn't a boring science book or a randor
coolest discoveries, the strangest history, and the craziest rea
that show how awesome (and weird) our world really is.

So get comfy, open your mind, and get ready to say "No way!" a few hundred times.

Let's dive in and discover the world's most mind-blowing facts — one fun page at a time.

Table of Contents

1. **Holiday Wonders** - Crazy, Cozy, and Totally Festive Facts!
   Discover surprising traditions, record-breaking snowmen, and weird holiday customs from around the world.
2. **Animal Kingdom**
   Explore the fascinating abilities, instincts, and secrets of animals from every corner of the planet.
3. **Space & the Universe**
   Learn mind-blowing facts about galaxies, stars, and the mysteries of outer space.
4. **Human Body & Mind**
   Uncover the hidden powers and strange quirks of the human body and brain.
5. **History's Hidden Secrets**
   Dive into unusual and forgotten moments that changed the course of history.
6. **Crazy Inventions & Tech**
   See how accidents, genius ideas, and futuristic technology have shaped our lives.
7. **World Records & Extremes**
   Meet the biggest, smallest, fastest, and most unusual achievements on Earth.
8. **Weird Food Facts**
   Discover strange, funny, and unbelievable facts about what we eat.
9. **Music, Movies & Pop Culture**
   Go behind the scenes of famous songs, films, and pop culture moments.
10. **Myths, Legends & Mysteries**
    Explore ancient tales, mysterious events, and stories that still can't be explained.
11. **Holiday & Festive Facts**
    Find out how people celebrate around the world in the weirdest and most wonderful ways.
12. **Famous People & Celebrities**
    Learn unexpected and little-known facts about the world's most recognizable names.

13. **The Internet & Social Media**
    Explore the digital world, from viral trends to the evolution of online culture.
14. **Sports & Games**
    Discover record-breaking plays, surprising athletes, and fun sports trivia.
15. **Fashion & Style**
    See how bold choices and wild trends have shaped the way we dress.
16. **Art & Creativity**
    Learn about remarkable works of art, strange performances, and creative breakthroughs.
17. **School & Learning Oddities**
    Strange facts about schools, teachers, and the curious ways we learn.
18. **Everyday Objects**
    The surprising origins and hidden secrets behind things we use every day.
19. **Weather & Natural Disasters**
    Explore the most powerful and unpredictable forces of nature on Earth.
20. **The Ocean & Underwater World**
    Dive deep into the secrets and wonders of the sea.
21. **Space Exploration & NASA**
    Incredible missions, discoveries, and milestones that expanded our reach into space.
22. **Ancient Civilizations**
    Discover lost cities, mysterious inventions, and ancient wisdom ahead of its time.
23. **Tiny vs. Giant**
    A look at the world's smallest and largest wonders, both natural and man-made.
24. **Time & Speed**
    Fascinating truths about how time moves, bends, and shapes our world.
25. **Human Emotions & Psychology**
    Understand what makes us feel, react, and think the way we do.
26. **Money & Business**
    Shocking and funny facts about fortunes, trade, and how money moves the world.

27. **The World's Strangest Laws**
    Real laws so unusual and funny, it's hard to believe they actually exist.
28. **War, Peace & Power**
    Unexpected stories, inventions, and moments born out of conflict and leadership.
29. **Future & Artificial Intelligence**
    A glimpse into the next era of robots, AI, and human innovation.
30. **Random But Awesome**
    A mix of fun, weird, and totally random facts that don't fit anywhere else.
31. **Strange Science**
    Discover surprising and unbelievable discoveries that challenge what we know about the world.
32. **Truths the World Ignored**
    Discover truths that were once rejected, ridiculed, or misunderstood.
33. **Ancient Mysteries & Lost Artifacts**
    Strange ancient objects and monuments that still puzzle scientists today.
34. **Lucky Breaks & Unexpected Successes**
    Real stories of incredible luck, chance, and success against all odds.
35. **Modern Legends & Viral Fame**
    The rise of internet fame, memes, and moments that defined online culture.
36. **American Politics & Presidents**
    Surprising and little-known facts about U.S. presidents and politics.
37. **Science vs. Beliefs**
    When science challenged superstition and changed how the world thinks.
38. **Unexplained Places & Phenomena**
    Mysterious locations and natural events that remain unsolved.
39. **Dumb Decisions with Big Consequences**
    Hilarious and strange mistakes that changed history in unexpected ways.
40. **The Planet's Weirdest Wonders**
    Explore Earth's most unbelievable natural formations and landscapes.
41. **The Celts** – Warriors, Wizards, and Ancient Mysteries

Chapter 1: Holiday Wonders
– Crazy, Cozy, and Totally Festive Facts!

The holidays are the most magical time of year — but also the strangest! Around the world, people celebrate with food fights, snow monsters, and goats made of straw.

From glowing deserts to Christmas trees in space, here are some of the wildest, warmest, and most wonderful holiday facts you've never heard before.

The world's largest snowman was over 120 feet tall.
Built in Maine, USA, she was named "Olympia" and had eyelashes made of skis.

In Japan, Christmas means fried chicken.
Families order KFC weeks in advance — it's considered a must-have holiday meal.

Iceland has 13 Santas — and a scary Christmas cat.
The Yule Lads leave treats in shoes, but the Yule Cat "eats" anyone who didn't get new clothes for Christmas.

In the Philippines, Christmas lasts four months.
Festivities begin in September and end in January — the longest holiday season on Earth.

Sweden builds a massive straw goat every year.
It's called the Gävle Goat — and pranksters have burned it down over 30 times.

In Spain, people eat 12 grapes at midnight for good luck.
One for each clock chime on New Year's Eve — but you have to finish them before the last bell.

In South Africa, fried caterpillars are a Christmas snack.
They're actually Emperor Moth larvae — crunchy and packed with protein.

"Jingle Bells" was written for Thanksgiving.
It was originally called "One Horse Open Sleigh" and had nothing to do with Christmas.

In Italy, a witch named La Befana delivers gifts.
She flies on a broomstick and gives candy to good kids and coal to naughty ones.

In Greece, people bake a coin into a New Year's cake.
Whoever finds it in their slice is said to have good luck all year.

The first artificial Christmas trees were made of goose feathers.
They were dyed green and imported from Germany in the 1800s.

In Denmark, people jump off chairs at midnight.
It's their way to "leap" into the new year with luck and joy.

The coldest Christmas ever recorded was -64°F in Siberia.
Frost covered everything — even eyelashes froze instantly.

The world's largest snow maze covered over three acres.
Built in Canada, it took weeks to finish and included ice slides and tunnels.

The first Advent calendars didn't have chocolate.
They started as chalk marks on doors counting down to Christmas Eve.

Santa's reindeer would need to travel 1,800 miles per second
to visit every child on Christmas Eve — faster than any rocket ever made.

In Venezuela, people roller-skate to church.
Streets in Caracas are closed to cars so everyone can skate safely to morning mass.

In Ukraine, people decorate trees with fake spider webs.
It's believed to bring wealth and happiness for the new year.

In Thailand, elephants join Christmas parades.
They wear Santa hats and carry gifts for children.

The first Christmas card was sent in 1843.
It showed a family drinking wine — and caused controversy for encouraging "too much cheer."

Germans invented the Advent calendar.
The first printed ones appeared in the early 1900s with Bible verses instead of candy.

In Mexico, people carve radishes into tiny sculptures.
It's called *La Noche de los Rábanos* — The Night of the Radishes.

In Scotland, New Year's is called Hogmanay.
People sing "Auld Lang Syne" and swing giant fireballs to burn away bad luck.

Ethiopia celebrates Christmas in January.
It's called *Genna*, and people wear white robes and play a game similar to hockey.

The biggest Christmas stocking ever made was 168 feet long.
It could hold more than 1,000 presents.

There's a giant Christmas market inside a cave in the Netherlands.
It's filled with lights, stalls, and underground carols.

In Hawaii, Santa arrives by canoe.
He trades his sleigh for waves and greets kids on the beach.

Reindeer are real — and some actually glow.
Their eyes reflect light differently in winter, helping them see in the Arctic dark.

In Japan, Christmas cake is covered in strawberries and whipped cream.
It symbolizes happiness and is eaten on December 25th.

Astronauts have celebrated Christmas in space.
They've sung carols, floated gifts, and even hung stockings on the International Space Station.

In Antarctica, scientists decorate snow labs.
They make "trees" out of ice and hold ugly sweater contests.

In Catalonia, Spain, people include a "pooping log" in Christmas décor.
It's called *Caga Tió* — kids hit it with sticks to make it "drop" candy.

The world's largest Christmas dinner fed 23,000 people.
It was hosted in India and included over four tons of chicken curry.

Finland has an underground Christmas park called Santa's Village.
You can meet reindeer, cross the Arctic Circle, and send postcards from Santa's official post office.

In Peru, people settle arguments with friendly fistfights.
It's a tradition called *Takanakuy*, where grudges are cleared before the new year begins.

A dog once saved Christmas mail.
In Alaska, a husky sled team delivered gifts after the plane carrying presents crashed in a snowstorm.

The Rockefeller Center Christmas tree has 50,000 LED lights.
That's enough to power a small village for a week.

Polar bears don't actually hibernate on Christmas.
They stay awake all winter — especially the mothers caring for cubs.

Americans eat about 200 million candy canes every year.
If lined up end to end, they'd stretch around the Earth twice.

The holidays show that joy can look totally different everywhere — but the feeling is always the same. Whether you're skating to church, building snow giants, or eating grapes at midnight, what matters most is sharing laughter, kindness, and that little spark of wonder.

In Hawaii, Santa arrives by canoe.

Chapter 2: Animal Kingdom

Animals are full of secrets that make them seem almost magical. Some can change colors, others use tools, and a few even communicate like humans. From the deep ocean to the highest trees, the animal world is bursting with mind-blowing abilities that show just how wild nature can be.

Crows Can Hold Grudges
Crows remember human faces and can recognize people who have treated them badly. They've even been seen warning other crows about "mean" humans.

Elephants Comfort Each Other
When one elephant is upset, others will touch it gently with their trunks or make low rumbling sounds to calm it down — just like a hug.

Sea Otters Hold Hands While They Sleep
To keep from drifting apart in the water, sea otters grab each other's paws and float in groups called rafts.

Pigeons Can Do Math
Studies show that pigeons can understand numerical order and simple math problems, almost like preschool kids.

Axolotls Can Regrow Their Hearts
These adorable salamanders can regenerate entire limbs — and even parts of their hearts and brains — without scarring.

Dolphins Have Names
Each dolphin has a unique whistle that works like a name, and they call each other by mimicking that sound.

Octopuses Use Coconut Shells as Tools
Some octopuses collect coconut shells and use them as portable shelters to hide from predators.

Flamingos Are Born Gray
Their pink color comes from the pigments in the shrimp and algae they eat. Without them, they'd stay gray forever.

Goats Have Rectangular Pupils
Their unusual eyes give them a super-wide view, helping them spot predators sneaking up from almost any direction.

Tardigrades Can Survive in Space
These tiny "water bears" can endure radiation, freezing, and even the vacuum of space by going into a hibernation-like state.

Spiders Can "Fly" Using Electricity
Certain spiders release silk threads that interact with the Earth's electric field, allowing them to float through the air for miles.

Male Seahorses Give Birth
Unlike most animals, it's the male seahorse that carries the babies in a special pouch until they're ready to swim on their own.

Bees Recognize Human Faces
Bees can remember and recognize faces by combining features, using a process similar to how we do.

Cows Have Best Friends
Cows form close friendships and can become stressed when separated from their favorite companion.

Penguins Propose with Pebbles
Male penguins search for the perfect pebble to give to a female as a sign of love and commitment.

Snakes Can Sense Earthquakes
Snakes detect vibrations through the ground and often flee their burrows days before an earthquake happens.

Giraffes Barely Sleep
They only rest for about 30 minutes a day, taking quick naps to stay alert for predators.

Parrots Name Their Babies
Some parrot species give each chick a distinct call sound that becomes its personal "name."

Lobsters Communicate by Peeing
Lobsters release urine from glands near their eyes to send messages — especially during fights or mating.

Rats Can Laugh
When tickled or playing, rats make high-pitched sounds that scientists describe as laughter.

Owls Can Turn Their Heads Almost All the Way Around
Special blood vessels and bone structures let them rotate their heads 270 degrees without cutting off circulation.

Whales Have Belly Buttons
Like all mammals, whales are born with belly buttons — proof that even the largest animals start small.

Frogs Swallow with Their Eyes
Frogs push their food down their throats by blinking and pressing their eyes inward.

Clownfish Can Change Gender
If the dominant female in a group dies, a male will transform into a female to take her place.

Jellyfish Don't Have Brains
They use a simple nerve network to sense light, movement, and danger — and it works surprisingly well.

From clever crows to space-traveling water bears, animals prove that intelligence and adaptability come in all shapes and sizes. The more we learn about them, the more incredible the natural world becomes.

Pigeons Can Do Math.   There's a Planet Made of Diamonds.

Chapter 3: Space & the Universe

Space is the ultimate mystery — vast, beautiful, and full of surprises that even scientists are still trying to understand. From stars that sing to planets that rain diamonds, the universe is a mix of wonder and weirdness. Get ready to explore some of the most unbelievable, yet completely real, facts about the great beyond.

Space Smells Like Burnt Metal
Astronauts say that space has a scent similar to seared steak or hot metal, caused by high-energy vibrations mixing with the oxygen inside their suits.

There's a Planet Made of Diamonds
A planet called 55 Cancri e is believed to be covered in diamond-like carbon because of its extreme pressure and heat.

Stars Can Sing
Some stars make low-frequency vibrations that translate into sound waves — though space itself is silent, scientists can detect their "music" through data.

Neutron Stars Are Super Dense
A teaspoon of a neutron star would weigh about a billion tons. That's because the atoms inside are crushed tightly together after a massive star explodes.

You Could Fit Over a Million Earths Inside the Sun
The Sun is so huge that about 1.3 million Earths could fit inside it — and it still wouldn't feel crowded.

The Moon Is Slowly Leaving Us
Every year, the Moon drifts about 1.5 inches farther from Earth. Don't worry — it'll take billions of years before it makes a real difference.

Space Isn't Completely Silent
There's no air to carry sound, but scientists use radio waves to detect space "noise" — hums and pulses from stars, planets, and even black holes.

There's an Immortal Storm on Jupiter
Jupiter's Great Red Spot has been raging for at least 400 years. It's a giant hurricane twice the size of Earth that never seems to stop.

Black Holes Stretch Time
Close to a black hole, gravity is so strong that time actually slows down. The deeper you go, the slower time moves compared to the outside universe.

You Age Slower in Space
Astronauts orbiting Earth experience time slightly slower due to Einstein's

theory of relativity — meaning space travelers come back just a tiny bit younger.

Saturn Could Float on Water
If you could find a bathtub big enough, Saturn would float because it's mostly made of gas and is less dense than water.

There's a Planet That Rains Glass
HD 189733b has sideways winds up to 4,000 mph that blow molten glass across the atmosphere. Definitely not a place for a vacation.

Some Stars Are Older Than the Universe
Well, almost — certain stars appear older than our universe's estimated age, leaving scientists still puzzled about how that's possible.

Venus Spins Backward
Unlike most planets, Venus rotates in the opposite direction of its orbit, making its days longer than its years.

There Are Rogue Planets With No Suns
These "orphan" planets float freely through space without orbiting any star — just wandering in the dark forever.

You Can't Stand on Jupiter
Even though it looks solid, Jupiter is made of gas and liquid — there's no surface to stand on, only endless clouds and storms.

Mars Has the Tallest Volcano in the Solar System
Olympus Mons is three times taller than Mount Everest and so wide it could cover the entire state of Arizona.

Space Isn't Far Away
The edge of space, called the Kármán Line, is only about 62 miles above Earth — that's less than a one-hour drive straight up (if you could).

There's a Cold Spot in Space No One Can Explain
Astronomers have found a massive region of space that's mysteriously colder than everything around it — and nobody knows why.

The Universe Is Expanding Faster and Faster
Instead of slowing down, the universe's expansion is speeding up, possibly because of something called "dark energy," which scientists still can't fully explain.

The universe is a place of endless curiosity — beautiful, strange, and beyond imagination. Every discovery out there reminds us how tiny we are... and how much more there is to explore.

Chapter 4: Human Body & Mind

Your body is a walking science experiment — full of strange powers, hidden systems, and tricks that even scientists are still discovering. From glowing skin and super-strong stomach acid to a brain that creates entire worlds in dreams, the human body is both weird and wonderful. Get ready to be amazed by what's happening inside you right now!

Your Brain Creates Electricity
Every thought you have sends out tiny electrical signals. Together, your brain could power a small light bulb if you could harness it.

Your Stomach Acid Can Dissolve Metal
The acid in your stomach is strong enough to melt through razor blades, but your stomach's protective lining keeps it safe.

Humans Glow in the Dark
Our bodies naturally give off a faint bioluminescence, but it's too weak for our eyes to see. Scientists can detect it with special cameras.

You're Taller in the Morning
When you sleep, the discs between your spine expand. As the day goes on, gravity compresses them, making you slightly shorter by evening.

Your Brain Never Stops Working
Even when you're asleep, your brain stays active — sorting memories, solving problems, and even practicing skills you learned that day.

You Replace Your Skin Every Month
Your body sheds around 40,000 skin cells every minute. In about a month, you've completely replaced your outer layer of skin.

You Have a "Second Brain" in Your Gut
The enteric nervous system in your digestive tract contains over 100 million nerve cells. It helps control digestion and even affects your mood.

Your Heart Can Keep Beating Outside Your Body
Because it has its own electrical system, a heart can continue beating for a short time after being removed from the body — under the right conditions.

Dreams Help Your Brain Clean Itself
During deep sleep, your brain clears out toxins through a special fluid system called the glymphatic system.

You See Things Upside Down
Your eyes flip images upside down before sending them to your brain, which then turns them right-side up again.

You Have Tiny Mites Living on Your Face
Microscopic mites called *Demodex* live in your pores and eat dead skin cells — but don't worry, everyone has them.

You Can't Tickle Yourself
Your brain predicts the motion of your own hands, so it cancels out the surprise response that causes laughter.

You Blink About 15,000 Times a Day
That's enough blinking to keep your eyes moist and clear dust, without you even thinking about it.

Your Blood Travels Thousands of Miles a Day
Your heart pumps blood through a network of vessels long enough to circle the Earth more than twice.

Your Nose Can Remember 50,000 Scents
The human nose is surprisingly powerful — capable of identifying and recalling tens of thousands of different smells.

You Have a Dominant Eye
Just like being left- or right-handed, one of your eyes is slightly stronger and leads your vision.

Laughter Is Contagious
Hearing someone laugh triggers a response in your brain that makes you want to join in. It's how humans bond socially.

Your Brain Can Rewire Itself
Called neuroplasticity, your brain can form new connections and even change structure when you learn new things.

Goosebumps Are a Leftover Superpower
They helped our ancestors look bigger when scared. Today, they're just a funny reminder of our animal past.

Tears Come in Three Types
Humans produce basal tears (for moisture), reflex tears (for protection), and emotional tears — each with a slightly different chemical makeup.

Your Tongue Has a Unique Print
Like fingerprints, everyone's tongue pattern is different. It could even be used for ID someday.

Your Ears Never Stop Growing
Cartilage keeps expanding as you age, which is why older people often have larger ears and noses.

You're Mostly Empty Space
At the atomic level, 99.9999999% of your body is empty space — but electromagnetic forces make you feel solid.

Your Brain Uses 20% of Your Energy
Even though it's only about 2% of your body weight, your brain burns a huge portion of the calories you eat.

Your Body Has Gold Inside It
There's about 0.2 milligrams of gold in your body, mostly in your blood. It's not enough to get rich, though!

The human body is like the universe in miniature — complex, mysterious, and constantly changing. The more we learn about it, the more it feels like science fiction hiding in plain sight.

Laughter Is Contagious.

Chapter 5: History's Hidden Secrets

History isn't just dates and dusty books — it's full of unbelievable stories that sound like movie plots. From forgotten heroes and strange coincidences to inventions born by accident, history is packed with secrets hiding in plain sight. These are the moments that changed the world in ways most people never learned in school.

Napoleon Wasn't Actually Short
He was about 5'6", which was average for men of his time. Confusion came from differences between French and British measurements — and a bit of propaganda.

A Dead Body Won a Presidential Election
In 1872, Horace Greeley died before the results came in, but people still voted for him. He ended up getting electoral votes after his death.

The Eiffel Tower Was Meant to Be Temporary
It was supposed to be dismantled after 20 years, but people loved it so much that it became France's permanent symbol.

A Chicken Survived 18 Months Without a Head
In 1945, a farmer accidentally missed the vital part of the brain while chopping off a chicken's head. "Miracle Mike" lived for over a year, fed through an eyedropper.

Cleopatra Lived Closer to the Moon Landing Than to the Pyramids
She ruled Egypt around 2,000 years before the first moon landing — but over 2,500 years after the Great Pyramid was built.

Ancient Romans Used Urine to Do Laundry
They collected urine from public baths because the ammonia helped clean clothes. Talk about recycling!

The Great Fire of London Stopped the Plague
The fire destroyed so many rat-infested homes in 1666 that it helped wipe out the bubonic plague.

Einstein Was Offered the Presidency of Israel
In 1952, Israel asked Albert Einstein to become its second president. He politely declined, saying he wasn't good with people.

World War I Sparked the Invention of Plastic Surgery
Doctors created new medical techniques to rebuild soldiers' faces after devastating injuries, which led to modern reconstructive surgery.

The First Alarm Clock Could Only Ring Once a Day
In 1787, Levi Hutchins built a clock that went off at 4 a.m. — his personal wake-up time — and it couldn't be reset until the next day.

Ketchup Was Once Sold as Medicine
In the 1830s, people believed tomatoes could cure stomach problems, so ketchup was bottled as a "health tonic."

The Shortest War in History Lasted 38 Minutes
The Anglo-Zanzibar War of 1896 ended before most people could even finish breakfast.

Pirates Wore Eye Patches for a Smart Reason
They didn't wear them because they lost eyes — patches helped them see better when moving between bright sunlight and dark ship interiors.

George Washington Never Lived in the White House
It was still being built when he was president. John Adams was the first to live there.

A 12-Year-Old Invented the Modern Popsicle
Frank Epperson accidentally left a cup of soda mix outside overnight in 1905 — with a stick in it. The frozen treat became a hit.

Vikings Never Actually Wore Horned Helmets
That image came from 19th-century operas. Real Viking helmets were plain and practical, made for battle — not fashion.

A Typo Once Caused a Major Stock Market Crash
In 2005, a Japanese trader accidentally tried to sell shares worth billions instead of thousands, briefly crashing the Tokyo Stock Exchange.

The Leaning Tower of Pisa Leaned Before It Was Finished
Builders noticed the tilt halfway through construction, but they kept going anyway — which only made it worse.

The First Computer Bug Was a Real Bug
In 1947, engineers found an actual moth stuck inside a computer, causing it to malfunction. That's where the term "computer bug" came from.

A War Was Fought Over a Bucket
In 1325, two Italian cities went to war after soldiers stole a wooden bucket. It lasted 12 years.

A 15-Year-Old Helped Discover Pluto
Clyde Tombaugh, a self-taught teenager, discovered the dwarf planet Pluto in 1930 using a homemade telescope.

The First Selfie Was Taken in 1839
Robert Cornelius, a photography pioneer, took a self-portrait by removing his camera's lens cap, running into frame, and holding still for several minutes.

Winston Churchill's Mother Was American
Jennie Jerome, born in Brooklyn, married into British high society — her son became one of the most famous leaders in history.

A Pigeon Won a War Medal
During World War I, a pigeon named Cher Ami delivered a lifesaving message despite being shot and badly injured, saving nearly 200 soldiers.

History isn't just what's written in textbooks — it's full of wild accidents, forgotten heroes, and moments too strange to make up. The past might be old, but it's never boring.

A Pigeon Won a War Medal.

The First Computer Bug Was a Real Bug.

Chapter 6: Crazy Inventions & Tech

From weird mistakes that changed the world to mind-blowing tech that feels straight out of science fiction, inventions have a way of surprising us. Some were created on purpose, others completely by accident — but all of them shaped how we live today. Get ready for a mix of genius, luck, and total weirdness in the world of technology.

Potato Chips Were Invented Out of Spite
A chef named George Crum made extra-thin fried potatoes in 1853 to annoy a complaining customer. Instead, the customer loved them — and chips were born.

Post-it Notes Came from a Failed Glue Experiment
A scientist trying to make super-strong glue accidentally created one that was weak but reusable. His colleague realized it was perfect for sticky notes.

Bubble Wrap Was Supposed to Be Wallpaper
Inventors originally designed Bubble Wrap as textured plastic wallpaper. It flopped in home decor but became a packaging legend.

Microwaves Were Discovered by Accident
A scientist working with radar noticed that a candy bar in his pocket melted from radiation. That led to the invention of the microwave oven.

The Internet Was Meant for Scientists, Not Memes
The original goal of the internet was to let researchers share data easily — no one imagined it would become a hub for cat videos.

Velcro Was Inspired by Burrs
After a walk with his dog, Swiss engineer George de Mestral studied the burrs stuck in its fur. Their tiny hooks inspired the invention of Velcro.

The First 3D Printer Was Made in the 1980s
Decades before they became popular, scientists were already printing plastic prototypes layer by layer using light.

Your Smartphone Is More Powerful Than the First Moon Computer
The computer that took Apollo 11 to the Moon was weaker than a modern calculator. Your phone could run thousands of those missions at once.

The Inventor of the Pringles Can Is Buried in One
Fred Baur, who designed the iconic can, loved his creation so much that part of his ashes were placed inside one when he died.

Google Started as a College Project
Larry Page and Sergey Brin created Google in a dorm room at Stanford University to organize the internet — now it practically *is* the internet.

A Teen Invented the Trampoline
In 1934, 16-year-old George Nissen got the idea for a "bouncing rig" after watching circus acrobats land in safety nets.

Artificial Intelligence Can Paint and Write Songs
AI programs can now create realistic art, compose music, and even write poetry — though some of it still sounds a little robotic.

The First Computer Mouse Was Made of Wood
In 1964, Douglas Engelbart built the first mouse from a wooden shell and two metal wheels. It was big, clunky, and revolutionary.

The Creator of Tetris Made It to Test Computer Power
Alexey Pajitnov designed the game in 1984 to check how well his software could handle patterns — and ended up creating a global obsession.

Nintendo Started by Selling Playing Cards
Long before video games, Nintendo made handmade playing cards in Japan. It didn't become a gaming company until nearly 80 years later.

A Scientist Accidentally Invented Safety Glass
In 1903, a chemist dropped a glass flask coated with plastic — and it didn't shatter. That mistake led to modern car windshields.

Robots Can Learn From YouTube Videos
Some robots are trained by watching videos of humans performing tasks, copying movements to learn how to cook or fold laundry.

Wi-Fi Was Inspired by a Movie Star
Actress Hedy Lamarr helped invent a radio system during World War II that later became the foundation for modern Wi-Fi and Bluetooth.

Someone Made a Working Jetpack for Real
Modern jetpacks can fly for several minutes using powerful engines — though they're loud, expensive, and still not ready for daily commutes.

People Used to Think X-Rays Could Cure Everything
In the early 1900s, X-ray machines were sold as miracle health devices — until doctors realized too much exposure was dangerous.

A 15-Year-Old Invented a Better Cancer Test
Jack Andraka created a paper sensor that can detect pancreatic cancer faster and cheaper than traditional tests — all from a high school science fair project.

Your Fingerprint Unlocking Feature Came From Spy Tech
Biometric scanning was originally developed for government security before becoming part of your phone's daily routine.

The First Email Was Sent to... Himself
In 1971, Ray Tomlinson sent the first email — to himself — just to test the system. It simply said something like "QWERTYUIOP."

There's a Robot That Can Draw Portraits
Named Ai-Da, this robot can sketch lifelike pictures using cameras and algorithms. She's even had her own art exhibitions.

The First 3D Movie Was Made in the 1920s
People were experimenting with 3D films almost a century ago, using red and blue lenses to create depth — long before modern 3D glasses.

Inventions prove that curiosity, mistakes, and a little imagination can change everything. Whether it's a teenage genius or a random accident, every great idea starts with someone asking, "What if?"

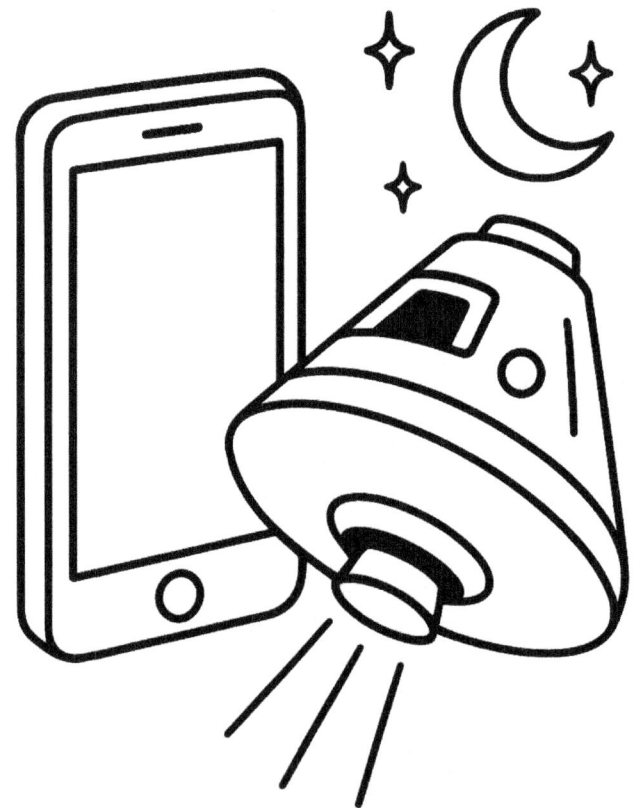

Your Smartphone Is More Powerful Than the First Moon Computer.

Chapter 7: World Records & Extremes

The world is full of incredible records — from the fastest humans to the tiniest creatures, the hottest places, and the weirdest achievements you can imagine. Some records were set through hard work, others by pure luck, and a few are so strange you'll wonder how anyone thought to try them. Let's dive into the biggest, smallest, longest, and wildest extremes ever recorded!

The Tallest Building Is Over Half a Mile High
The Burj Khalifa in Dubai stands at 2,717 feet tall — that's taller than three Eiffel Towers stacked on top of each other.

The Fastest Animal Is the Peregrine Falcon
This bird can dive at over 240 miles per hour — faster than a race car on a Formula 1 track.

The World's Smallest Mammal Fits on a Finger
The bumblebee bat from Thailand weighs less than a penny and could easily nap inside a teaspoon.

The Hottest Temperature Ever Recorded Was in California
Death Valley reached 134°F in 1913 — it's so hot that shoes can melt on the pavement.

The World's Longest Pizza Stretched Over a Mile
In California, chefs teamed up to bake a pizza 1.3 miles long using over 17,000 pounds of dough.

The Oldest Tree Is Older Than the Pyramids
A bristlecone pine in California is nearly 5,000 years old — it sprouted before the Great Pyramid of Giza was built.

The Deepest Point on Earth Could Swallow Mount Everest
The Mariana Trench in the Pacific Ocean is about 36,000 feet deep. If you dropped Mount Everest inside, it would still be underwater.

The Largest Snowflake Ever Measured Was 15 Inches Wide
It fell in Montana in 1887 — that's bigger than a dinner plate.

The Longest Word in English Has 189,819 Letters
It's the chemical name for "titin," a massive protein in the human body. Saying it out loud would take over three hours.

The World's Fastest Roller Coaster Hits 150 mph
Formula Rossa in Abu Dhabi launches riders faster than most airplanes take off.

The Heaviest Pumpkin Weighed More Than a Small Car
A farmer in Italy grew a pumpkin that tipped the scales at 2,702 pounds — the size of a mini sedan.

The Longest Fingernails Ever Were Over 28 Feet Combined
An American woman, Ayanna Williams, grew her nails for nearly 30 years before finally cutting them.

The World's Largest Pizza Was Over 13,000 Square Feet
Made in Los Angeles in 2023, it used enough cheese to cover an entire basketball court.

The Fastest Typist Can Type Over 200 Words a Minute
With perfect accuracy, Barbara Blackburn once hit speeds faster than most people can read.

The World's Loudest Sound Could Be Heard 3,000 Miles Away
The 1883 eruption of Krakatoa was so loud that it shattered eardrums 40 miles from the volcano.

The Largest Animal Ever Is Alive Right Now
The blue whale is bigger than any dinosaur that ever lived. Its heart alone weighs as much as a car.

The Longest Living Animal Is a 500-Year-Old Clam
A clam nicknamed "Ming" was found to be over five centuries old — older than Shakespeare.

The Most Expensive Painting Ever Sold Cost $450 Million
Leonardo da Vinci's *Salvator Mundi* set the record in 2017 — that's enough money to buy a private island.

The World's Longest Flight Without Refueling Lasted Over 9 Days
In 1986, a plane called the Voyager circled the globe nonstop without landing once.

The Fastest Human Can Outrun a Hurricane (Almost)
Usain Bolt reached a top speed of 27.8 mph, just shy of the average speed of a tropical storm.

The Largest Swimming Pool Is Over Half a Mile Long
Located in Chile, it's so big that you can sail boats across it.

The Longest Book Ever Written Has Over 9 Million Words
A French novel called *Artamène ou le Grand Cyrus* was written in the 1600s and takes months to finish.

The Most Expensive Mistake Cost $370 Million
NASA lost a Mars orbiter because one team used metric units while another used inches — and the spacecraft crashed.

The Highest Jump by a Human Was Over 8 Feet
Cuban athlete Javier Sotomayor still holds the world record in the high jump — taller than the average ceiling.

From giant whales to lightning-fast falcons, the world is packed with extremes that stretch the limits of what's possible. Whether it's human effort or nature's power, there's always something that breaks the record — and then someone else trying to top it.

The Fastest Animal Is the Peregrine Falcon.

The World's Smallest Mammal Fits on a Finger.

Chapter 8: Weird Food Facts

Food isn't just fuel — it's full of wild stories, strange ingredients, and unexpected science. From snacks created by mistake to dishes that sound too crazy to be real, the world of food is packed with surprises. Get ready to rethink what's on your plate!

Ketchup Used to Be Made from Fish
Before tomatoes took over, early versions of ketchup in Asia were made from fermented fish sauce and spices.

Pineapples Take Almost Two Years to Grow
Each pineapple grows from a single plant and takes up to 24 months to fully ripen — that's a long wait for a smoothie.

Carrots Were Originally Purple
Before orange carrots became popular in the 1600s, most carrots were purple, yellow, or white.

Cheese Is Older Than Written History
Archaeologists found evidence of cheese-making from over 7,000 years ago — long before anyone invented writing.

Peanuts Aren't Nuts
They grow underground like beans, which makes them part of the legume family, not the nut family.

Honey Never Goes Bad
Because it has no moisture and natural acids, honey found in ancient Egyptian tombs is still safe to eat.

French Fries Aren't French
They were first made in Belgium, but American soldiers discovered them during World War I and brought the recipe home.

There's Gold in Chocolate
Some luxury chocolates are topped with real edible gold leaf — it doesn't taste like anything, but it sure looks fancy.

Wasabi Isn't Always Real Wasabi
Most wasabi served outside Japan is actually colored horseradish, because real wasabi is rare and expensive.

Cucumbers Are 96% Water
That's why they're so refreshing — eating one is almost like drinking a glass of water.

Popcorn Was Around Before Movie Theaters
Ancient civilizations in the Americas were eating popcorn thousands of years before movies even existed.

You Can Eat Glow-in-the-Dark Ice Cream
Scientists created ice cream using jellyfish protein that glows when you lick it — though it costs over $200 a scoop.

Pizza in Space Is a Real Thing
In 2001, Pizza Hut delivered a pizza to astronauts on the International Space Station. It cost over $1 million to send it there.

A Tomato Is Technically a Fruit, but the Law Says It's a Vegetable
In 1893, the U.S. Supreme Court ruled tomatoes should be taxed as vegetables because they're eaten with meals, not desserts.

Bananas Are All Clones
Nearly every banana you eat is genetically identical to every other one, which makes them vulnerable to diseases.

You Can Boil Water with Ice in Antarctica
At high altitudes and freezing temperatures, scientists have used ice and low pressure to make water boil.

The World's Most Expensive Coffee Comes from Animal Poop
It's called Kopi Luwak, made from coffee beans eaten and "processed" by a small animal called a civet.

Pasta Wasn't Invented in Italy
Early forms of pasta came from China and the Middle East long before Italians perfected it.

The Holes in Swiss Cheese Come from Bacteria "Burps"
Tiny gas bubbles form during fermentation, creating the classic cheese holes we know and love.

Ranch Dressing Is America's Favorite — by a Lot
Nearly half of all salad dressings sold in the U.S. are ranch. It's even used on pizza, fries, and burgers.

White Chocolate Isn't Really Chocolate
It doesn't contain cocoa solids — only cocoa butter, sugar, and milk — which gives it that sweet, creamy flavor.

Apples Float Because They're Full of Air
About 25% of an apple's volume is air, which makes them perfect for bobbing in Halloween games.

The Smell of Freshly Baked Bread Is a Brain Trick
It triggers memories and comfort feelings in your brain, which is why bakeries always smell irresistible.

Grapes Can Explode in the Microwave
When two grapes are heated close together, the plasma created between them can spark like lightning.

Nutmeg Can Be Dangerous in Large Amounts
Eating too much nutmeg can cause hallucinations because of a natural compound called myristicin.

From fishy ketchup to glowing desserts, food proves that the world's weirdest ideas can still taste amazing. So next time you eat, remember — there's probably a strange story hiding behind every bite.

Pizza in Space Is a Real Thing.

Apples Float Because They're Full of Air.

Chapter 9: Music, Movies & Pop Culture

Pop culture never stands still — it's a mix of wild creativity, lucky accidents, and unforgettable moments that shape what we watch, listen to, and talk about. From the secrets behind hit songs to strange celebrity facts and movie mistakes that became iconic, these stories prove that fame is often stranger than fiction.

The Beatles Couldn't Read Music
Despite being one of the most famous bands ever, none of the Beatles could actually read sheet music. They played entirely by ear.

A Teen Wrote "Rolling in the Deep" After a Breakup
Adele was only 21 when she turned heartbreak into one of the most powerful songs of all time.

"Let It Go" Was Written in a Single Day
The Frozen hit that kids (and parents) couldn't stop singing was written in about eight hours by husband-and-wife songwriters.

Elvis Presley Never Wrote His Own Songs
He was known as the King of Rock 'n' Roll, but every song he sang was written by someone else.

Billie Eilish Recorded Her First Album in a Bedroom
Her breakout album, *When We All Fall Asleep, Where Do We Go?*, was made with her brother Finneas in their Los Angeles home.

Taylor Swift Wrote Her First Hit at Age 14
She wrote "Tim McGraw" while still in high school — proving that some careers really do start early.

Michael Jackson's Moonwalk Wasn't His Idea
He learned the move from street dancers and turned it into a legendary part of pop history.

"Shrek" Almost Starred a Completely Different Voice
Chris Farley originally voiced Shrek, but after his death, Mike Myers re-recorded all the lines — in a Scottish accent that became iconic.

The "Star Wars" Lightsaber Sound Came from a TV Set
The famous hum was created by mixing the sound of a film projector and a buzzing old TV.

Pixar Movies All Exist in the Same Universe
Fans discovered hidden Easter eggs that connect every Pixar film — from *Toy Story* to *Finding Nemo* to *Monsters, Inc.*

"The Lion King" Was Almost Canceled
Disney thought the movie would flop, focusing instead on *Pocahontas*. It went on to become one of their biggest hits ever.

Drake Once Played a Teen in a Wheelchair
Before becoming a rap superstar, Drake starred in the Canadian TV show *Degrassi: The Next Generation*.

Beyoncé Has an Alter Ego Named Sasha Fierce
She created the persona to help her perform more confidently on stage — a bold, fearless version of herself.

Kanye West Made Beats for Jay-Z Before Becoming Famous
Before his solo career, Kanye was a producer who helped create Jay-Z's hit *Izzo (H.O.V.A.)*.

"Harry Potter" Almost Had a Different Name in the U.S.
Publishers wanted to rename it *Harry Potter and the School of Magic* because they thought "Philosopher's Stone" sounded too serious.

Marvel Filmed Multiple Fake Scenes to Prevent Spoilers
During *Avengers: Endgame*, actors got different versions of the script so no one knew how it really ended.

Lady Gaga Was Dropped by Her First Record Label
Before becoming a superstar, her first label told her she'd "never make it" — they were very wrong.

The "i" in iPhone Doesn't Mean "Internet"
Apple said it stands for "individual," "instruct," "inform," and "inspire" — not just "internet."

Post Malone Got His Stage Name from a Rap Name Generator
He entered his real name, Austin Post, into an online generator — and "Post Malone" stuck for life.

One of the First Memes Was From the 1920s
A cartoon called "Expectations vs. Reality" went viral in newspapers a century before the internet existed.

The Longest Movie Ever Made Is Over 35 Days Long
A Swedish film called *Logistics* shows the journey of a product from start to finish — in real time.

Rihanna's Umbrella Was Originally Meant for Britney Spears
The song was offered to several artists before Rihanna turned it into a global hit.

A Fan Once Sent Taylor Swift a Real Turtle
She's received thousands of gifts from fans — but a live animal was one of the weirdest.

Netflix Started as a Late Fee Complaint
The founder got the idea after being charged $40 for returning a movie late — and decided to create a service with no late fees ever again.

Pop culture keeps reinventing itself, turning mistakes into hits and accidents into legends. Whether it's a song recorded in a bedroom or a movie that almost didn't happen, creativity has no rules — and that's what makes it unforgettable.

The "Star Wars" Lightsaber Sound Came from a TV Set.

Chapter 10: Myths, Legends & Mysteries

Some stories never die — from ancient myths to unexplained mysteries, the world is full of strange events that blur the line between fact and fiction. Whether it's weird disappearances, mythical creatures, or unsolved secrets that scientists still can't explain, these tales continue to fascinate us because... what if they're true?

The Bermuda Triangle Might Not Be That Mysterious
Many "disappearances" blamed on the Bermuda Triangle were later explained by storms, compass errors, and human mistakes — but the legend still sails on.

Atlantis Might Have Been Real — Sort Of
Some historians think the myth of Atlantis came from stories about real ancient cities destroyed by volcanic eruptions or tsunamis.

The Loch Ness Monster Could Be a Giant Eel
Scientists tested the lake's DNA and found traces of eels much larger than expected — maybe not Nessie, but still pretty creepy.

Stonehenge Was Built Before the Pyramids
The famous rock circle in England was built over 5,000 years ago, and no one knows exactly how people moved those huge stones without modern tools.

People Still Don't Know Who Built the Pyramids' Inner Chambers
While Egyptians built the pyramids, the methods for creating the narrow tunnels and secret rooms inside remain a mystery.

A Meteor May Have Started the Legend of the Holy Grail
Some researchers think the "cup from heaven" in Arthurian legend was inspired by ancient stories about meteorites falling to Earth.

The Lost Colony of Roanoke Just... Vanished
An English settlement in the 1500s disappeared completely, leaving behind only the word "CROATOAN" carved into a post.

There's a Real "Mummy's Curse" — Kind Of
When King Tut's tomb was opened in 1922, several people involved died mysteriously, likely from ancient mold spores, not magic.

Bigfoot Sightings Happen on Every Continent Except Antarctica
Thousands of reports describe giant, hairy humanoids — though none have ever been proven. Maybe Bigfoot just hates the cold.

The Nazca Lines Can Only Be Seen from the Sky
These massive drawings in Peru look like animals and shapes — but ancient people made them long before humans could fly.

UFOs Are Officially Called "UAPs" Now
The U.S. government renamed them "Unidentified Aerial Phenomena" and even released real military videos of flying objects no one can explain.

The Tunguska Explosion Flattened a Forest but Left No Crater
In 1908, something exploded over Siberia with the force of hundreds of atomic bombs — but no meteor was ever found.

The Voynich Manuscript Is Written in an Unknown Language
This centuries-old book is filled with strange drawings and mysterious text that no one has ever been able to decode.

There's a "Door to Hell" Burning in the Desert
A massive gas crater in Turkmenistan has been burning non-stop since 1971 after scientists accidentally set it on fire.

Easter Island Statues Have Bodies Underground
The famous giant heads actually have full bodies buried under layers of earth and rock.

A Real "Zombie" Fungus Controls Insects
The Ophiocordyceps fungus infects ants' brains and forces them to climb high before taking over their bodies — creepy but true.

Ancient Myths May Have Predicted Real Disasters
Stories of great floods, like Noah's Ark, might come from memories of real floods after the Ice Age.

People Still Hear Sounds from the Deep Ocean That No One Can Identify
NOAA scientists have recorded mysterious noises, like "The Bloop," that could come from huge unknown sea creatures — or something else.

A Giant City Might Exist Under the Amazon Jungle
Modern mapping technology has revealed hidden networks of ancient roads and villages deep in the rainforest.

Some People Believe Time Travelers Left Clues in Old Photos
Photos showing "modern" clothing or objects from the past have fueled wild theories — though most turn out to be coincidences.

A 2,000-Year-Old Computer Was Found in the Ocean
The Antikythera Mechanism, discovered in a shipwreck, could predict eclipses and planetary movements — way ahead of its time.

The Mary Celeste Was Found Floating with No Crew
In 1872, the ship was discovered perfectly intact with meals still on the table — but the entire crew had vanished.

There's a Hidden Room Behind Mount Rushmore
A secret chamber was built behind Lincoln's head to store important documents, but it was never completed.

A Mysterious "Hum" Drives Some People Crazy
In certain towns, residents report hearing a constant low-pitched hum — but no one can find its source.

The Pyramids of Egypt Line Up Perfectly with the Stars
The Great Pyramids match the pattern of Orion's Belt — proof of ancient astronomy skills, or something more mysterious?

From lost cities to eerie sounds and vanishing ships, the world's mysteries remind us how much we still don't know. Some secrets might never be solved — and that's what keeps them so exciting.

The Loch Ness Monster Could Be a Giant Eel.

Bigfoot Sightings Happen on Every Continent Except Antarctica.

Chapter 11: Holiday & Festive Facts

Holidays bring out the weirdest and most wonderful traditions around the world. From flying witches and pickle ornaments to fireworks made of sugar, people celebrate in ways you'd never expect. Some customs are ancient, others are brand-new — but all of them prove that humans will find *any* excuse to have fun.

Japan Eats KFC for Christmas Dinner
Every Christmas, millions of people in Japan line up to buy fried chicken — thanks to a 1970s marketing campaign that turned KFC into a holiday tradition.

In Iceland, Cats Judge Your Fashion Choices
The Yule Cat is a giant monster that supposedly eats people who don't get new clothes for Christmas. Time to appreciate those socks!

New Year's in Spain Starts with Grapes
Spaniards eat 12 grapes at midnight — one for each clock chime — to bring good luck for every month of the new year.

Sweden Has a Giant Straw Goat That Keeps Getting Burned Down
Every December, the city of Gävle builds a massive straw goat, but pranksters often set it on fire — it's practically part of the tradition.

In Germany, Kids Hunt for a Pickle Ornament
Parents hide a pickle-shaped ornament on the Christmas tree, and the first child to find it gets an extra present.

In Italy, a Witch Brings the Gifts
Instead of Santa Claus, Italians celebrate La Befana — a kind old witch who delivers sweets on her broomstick every January 6th.

Easter in Australia Has a Bunny Rival
To protect crops, Australians created the Easter Bilby, a cute marsupial, to replace the traditional (and invasive) Easter Bunny.

Norway Hides Its Brooms on Christmas Eve
According to old legends, witches steal brooms to fly on Christmas night — so people hide them before they can take off.

The World's Largest Snow Maze Is in Canada
Every winter, Manitoba builds a snow maze covering over 30,000 square feet — that's bigger than six basketball courts.

In the Philippines, Christmas Starts in September
The "Ber Months" (September–December) are full of carols, lights, and parties — making it the longest Christmas season on Earth.

Finland Has a National "Day of the Sauna"
On Christmas Eve, Finnish families relax in a sauna before celebrating — it's a time to warm up and reflect before the big feast.

Thailand's Water Festival Turns Cities into Splash Zones
During Songkran, people celebrate the New Year by soaking each other with buckets, hoses, and water guns in giant street battles.

In Austria, Santa Has a Scary Friend
Krampus, a horned creature, follows Saint Nicholas and punishes naughty kids — basically the opposite of Christmas cheer.

Halloween Was Born in Ireland
The ancient Celtic festival of Samhain celebrated the end of harvest — with bonfires, costumes, and stories about spirits. Sound familiar?

People in Ecuador Burn "Bad Luck Dolls" on New Year's Eve
Families make dolls that represent the bad things from the past year and burn them at midnight to start fresh.

The First Thanksgiving Lasted Three Days
In 1621, the Pilgrims and the Wampanoag tribe celebrated their harvest feast for an entire long weekend.

China's Lantern Festival Marks the End of New Year Celebrations
Thousands of glowing lanterns light up the night sky, symbolizing hope, wishes, and the return of spring.

In Venezuela, People Roller-Skate to Church
In the capital city, streets close on Christmas morning so families can skate safely to early mass.

Valentine's Day Once Included Friendship Cards
In the 1800s, people didn't just send romantic notes — they mailed "friendship valentines" to their best pals, too.

New Year's Fireworks Started in Ancient China
Fireworks were invented over a thousand years ago to scare away evil spirits and welcome good fortune.

Scotland's New Year Is Called Hogmanay
One of the biggest celebrations in the world, Hogmanay includes bonfires, singing "Auld Lang Syne," and even swinging fireballs.

Mexico's Day of the Dead Isn't About Sadness
Families celebrate loved ones who've passed away with colorful altars, food, and parades — it's a joyful festival of remembrance.

In Greece, People Hang Onions on Their Doors for Good Luck
The onion's power to sprout again symbolizes rebirth and growth for the new year.

The World's Largest Easter Egg Was 31 Feet Tall
Built in Canada in 1975, the massive egg (called a pysanka) was made from thousands of aluminum pieces.

Some Japanese Couples Celebrate Christmas Like Valentine's Day
It's more about romance than religion — with lights, dates, and fancy cakes instead of family dinners.

Holidays show how creative — and weird — humans can be when it comes to celebrating life. No matter where you are in the world, there's always a reason to decorate, dance, or share something sweet.

The World's Largest Snow Maze Is in Canada.

Chapter 12: Famous People & Celebrities

We know celebrities for their music, movies, and fame — but behind the spotlight, they're full of surprises. Some stars have bizarre hobbies, strange phobias, or past jobs you'd never guess. Get ready to see your favorite celebs in a whole new (and way funnier) light.

Dwayne "The Rock" Johnson Used to Sleep on a Mattress He Found in the Street
Before becoming one of Hollywood's highest-paid actors, The Rock struggled with money and lived in tiny apartments with secondhand furniture.

Billie Eilish's First Song Was About Zombies
She wrote her first song at age 11 after watching an episode of *The Walking Dead*.

Tom Holland Found Out He Got the Role of Spider-Man From Instagram
Marvel accidentally posted the news online before officially telling him — talk about spoilers!

Taylor Swift Grew Up on a Christmas Tree Farm
Before she was selling out stadiums, she was helping her family sell holiday trees every winter.

Ed Sheeran Once Slept on a Friend's Couch for Two Years
Before fame, he didn't have a home — he crashed on friends' couches while performing small gigs around London.

Katy Perry Started as a Gospel Singer
Her first album was Christian music before she switched to pop and became a global star.

Beyoncé Has an Alter Ego Named "Sasha Fierce"
She invented the persona to help her overcome stage fright and perform more confidently.

Keanu Reeves Secretly Gives Away Most of His Movie Salary
He's known for donating millions to children's hospitals and the film crew — he says money doesn't make him happy.

Rihanna's Real Name Isn't Rihanna
Her full name is Robyn Rihanna Fenty — she just uses her middle name as her stage name.

Harry Styles Loves to Bake
When he's not touring, the pop star relaxes by baking bread and desserts — he's even joked about opening a bakery.

Zendaya Means "To Give Thanks" in Shona
Her name comes from the African language of Zimbabwe and perfectly fits her positive personality.

Leonardo DiCaprio Was Named After a Painting
His mom decided on the name when she felt him kick while standing in front of a Leonardo da Vinci painting.

Lady Gaga's Stage Name Came From a Queen Song
Her producer texted "Radio Ga Ga," and autocorrect shortened it — creating one of the most famous stage names ever.

Ariana Grande's Favorite Animal Is a Pig
She even adopted a pet pig named Piggy Smallz, who sometimes appears in her videos.

Tom Cruise Is Afraid of Heights — But Does His Own Stunts
Even though he's scared, he still insists on doing dangerous stunts himself, including hanging off airplanes.

Selena Gomez Has Her Own Ice Cream Flavor
She partnered with a famous brand to create "Cookies & Cream Remix," inspired by one of her favorite desserts.

Elon Musk Once Sold a Video Game He Coded at Age 12
He created a space-themed game called *Blastar* and sold it for $500 when he was still in middle school.

Emma Watson Graduated from Brown University
Even with her acting career, she still made time to earn a degree in English literature from an Ivy League school.

Post Malone Loves Crocs So Much, He Designed His Own Line
His collab shoes sold out in minutes — proving that comfort *is* cool.

Justin Bieber Can Solve a Rubik's Cube in Under Two Minutes
He learned the trick during his early tours and often shows off the skill in interviews.

Oprah Winfrey's First Job Was at a Grocery Store
She worked bagging groceries before starting her broadcasting career and becoming a billionaire.

Ryan Reynolds Bought a Soccer Team
He co-owns Wrexham AFC, a small Welsh club that gained global fame thanks to his hilarious social media posts.

Miley Cyrus's Real Name Isn't Miley
She was born Destiny Hope Cyrus — "Miley" came from her childhood nickname "Smiley."

Adele Almost Became a Music Teacher Instead of a Singer
Before her big break, she planned to teach kids how to sing — but her demo went viral first.

Zendaya Helped Design Some of Her Red Carpet Dresses
She loves fashion so much that she often sketches and helps create her own looks.

Johnny Depp Owns His Own Island
He bought a private island in the Bahamas — and uses solar panels to power it because he's big on sustainability.

Fame might look perfect from the outside, but even the biggest stars have humble beginnings, weird hobbies, and funny backstories. It just proves that no matter how famous you are, everyone's got their quirks — and that's what makes them unforgettable.

Ariana Grande's Favorite Animal Is a Pig.

Chapter 13: The Internet & Social Media

The internet never sleeps — it's a nonstop world of memes, viral videos, and digital revolutions. From the first-ever website to billion-view TikToks, the online world has changed how we live, talk, and even think. It's funny, fast, and sometimes totally bizarre — just like the people who use it.

The First-Ever Website Is Still Online
Launched in 1991, the very first website was about how to use the World Wide Web — and you can still visit it today.

The "@" Symbol Is Over 500 Years Old
It wasn't created for emails. Merchants in the 1500s used it to mean "at the rate of" when calculating prices.

Google Was Almost Named "Backrub"
Before becoming the world's biggest search engine, the founders called it "Backrub" because it analyzed website links — like the internet's "backbone."

The First YouTube Video Was About Elephants
In 2005, YouTube co-founder Jawed Karim uploaded *Me at the Zoo,* a 19-second clip that started the world's biggest video platform.

The Most-Liked Photo on Instagram Is an Egg
A simple picture of an egg broke the internet in 2019, beating Kylie Jenner's record with over 55 million likes.

TikTok Wasn't Originally Called TikTok
It started in China as an app called Douyin, and when it expanded globally, the name changed to TikTok — like the ticking of a clock.

Someone Once Sold a GIF for Half a Million Dollars
A digital artwork called "Nyan Cat" — a rainbow cat flying through space — sold as an NFT for over $500,000 in 2021.

Hashtags Were Invented by Accident
In 2007, a Twitter user suggested using "#" to group topics, and the idea caught on instantly — now hashtags are everywhere.

Wikipedia Has More Pages Than Any Encyclopedia in History
With over six million English-language articles, Wikipedia grows by hundreds of new pages every day.

The Average Teen Scrolls About Five Miles a Year on Their Phone
Add up all those little thumb swipes, and you're literally scrolling the distance of a marathon each year.

Twitter's Bird Has a Name
The blue bird logo is actually named "Larry" — after basketball legend Larry Bird.

Facebook's First Name Was "Thefacebook"
When it launched in 2004, it was only for Harvard students — and "The" was later dropped for simplicity.

Reddit Is Known as "The Front Page of the Internet"
With millions of active communities, Reddit covers everything from science to memes — and sometimes breaks major news before TV does.

Memes Go Back to the 1970s
The word "meme" was invented by scientist Richard Dawkins in 1976 to describe how ideas spread — long before Pepe or Doge.

The "Rickroll" Meme Started as a Prank in 2007
It began when users clicked what they thought was a cool link — only to be greeted by Rick Astley's *Never Gonna Give You Up*.

Google Earth Once Revealed a Hidden Rainforest Tribe
In 2008, satellite images spotted a group of people in the Amazon who had never made contact with the outside world.

Some People Have Made a Living Playing Video Games
Professional gamers and streamers can earn millions — all from entertaining others online.

The Word "Spam" Comes From a Canned Meat Commercial
It became internet slang after a Monty Python sketch where everyone kept yelling "Spam!" nonstop.

The Longest Wi-Fi Connection Spanned Over 200 Miles
Engineers in Italy managed to transmit a Wi-Fi signal across the ocean — farther than most people drive in a day.

YouTube Was Originally a Dating Site
Its founders planned it as a place to upload "video dating profiles," but no one used it that way — so they switched to general videos.

Someone Once Tried to Name Their Child "@"
A Chinese couple attempted it to show their love for technology — officials said no.

The First-Ever Tweet Was "Just Setting Up My Twttr"
Posted by Twitter co-founder Jack Dorsey in 2006, it later sold as an NFT for over $2.9 million.

Snapchat's Original Name Was "Picaboo"
The app was launched in 2011 to send disappearing photos — but the name changed after a legal dispute.

The Internet Weighs as Much as a Strawberry
If you measured all the electrons that store data online, their combined mass would weigh about the same as one strawberry.

The Word "Google" Became a Verb in 2006
It officially entered the Oxford English Dictionary that year — meaning "to search for something online."

The World's First Email Was Sent to... Himself
Ray Tomlinson tested the system in 1971 by sending himself a message that said something like "QWERTYUIOP."

The "@" Symbol Is Over 500 Years Old.

Chapter 14: Sports & Games

Sports aren't just about winning — they're about insane records, wild traditions, and moments so weird they sound made up. From underwater hockey to marathon runners who fell asleep mid-race, the world of sports is packed with stories that prove athletes are just as creative as they are competitive. Get ready for some jaw-dropping plays and unbelievable trivia!

The Olympics Used to Include Art Competitions
From 1912 to 1948, artists could win Olympic medals for painting, music, and sculpture — as long as their work was sports-themed.

Basketball Was Invented by a Gym Teacher With a Peach Basket
In 1891, Dr. James Naismith nailed a peach basket to a gym wall to keep students active during winter — and the rest is history.

A Golf Ball Once Landed on the Moon
Astronaut Alan Shepard hit two golf balls on the moon during the Apollo 14 mission in 1971. One supposedly traveled for miles in low gravity.

The First Baseball Game Was Played With No Gloves
In the 1800s, players caught fastballs with bare hands. Gloves were later added to prevent constant injuries.

The Longest Tennis Match Lasted Over 11 Hours
In 2010, John Isner and Nicolas Mahut battled for three days at Wimbledon, with Isner finally winning 70–68 in the fifth set.

The World's Largest Game of Hide-and-Seek Had Over 2,000 Players
It took place in Italy in 2015 and turned an entire mountain village into a massive playground.

A Soccer Player Once Got a Yellow Card for Celebrating Too Much
After scoring, he jumped into the crowd to celebrate — the referee called it "excessive happiness."

The Fastest Baseball Pitch Ever Thrown Hit 105.1 mph
Aroldis Chapman set the record in 2010, throwing a pitch faster than most cars on the highway.

Table Tennis Balls Used to Be Made of Celluloid
The material was so flammable that some matches literally caught fire during rallies.

There's a Real Sport Called Chess Boxing
It's exactly what it sounds like — players alternate between rounds of chess and boxing until one wins by checkmate or knockout.

Sumo Wrestlers Eat Around 7,000 Calories a Day
Their special stew, called chanko-nabe, helps them gain massive muscle and weight for matches.

The FIFA World Cup Trophy Was Once Stolen — and Found by a Dog
In 1966, a dog named Pickles discovered the missing trophy wrapped in newspaper in a London garden.

Bowling Used to Be Illegal in England
In the 1300s, King Edward III banned it because soldiers were skipping archery practice to play.

Michael Phelps Has More Gold Medals Than 161 Countries
The Olympic swimmer's 23 golds outshine the total gold count of many nations combined.

The Longest Running Race Ever Covered 3,100 Miles
The "Self-Transcendence Run" in New York lasts nearly two months — runners circle a single city block thousands of times.

There's a Soccer Team in England That's Older Than the Country's Laws
Sheffield FC, founded in 1857, is the oldest football club in the world — older than the official rulebook.

A Professional Hockey Game Once Ended With a Score of 0–0
Both goalies made over 70 saves each, proving that sometimes defense *is* more exciting than offense.

The NBA's Shortest Player Could Dunk
Muggsy Bogues stood only 5'3" but still managed to dunk during his time in the league — talk about vertical power.

A Horse Once Competed in the Olympics
In 1900, an equestrian named Constant van Langendonck entered his horse in a long jump event — without a rider.

The Most Popular Sport in the World Isn't Soccer — Technically
By participation, fishing has more global players than any organized sport.

There's an Underwater Version of Rugby
Played in a swimming pool, players wear flippers and snorkels while trying to get the ball into a weighted goal.

Baseball Umpires Used to Sit Behind the Catcher in a Rocking Chair
In the sport's early days, the "judge" watched plays comfortably from a chair — until someone realized that might not be ideal.

The Fastest Marathon Ever Was Run at a 4:34 Per Mile Pace
Eliud Kipchoge broke the two-hour barrier in 2019, running an entire marathon faster than most people can sprint for a block.

Video Games Are Now an Official Medal Event
The 2023 Olympic Esports Week marked the first time gaming joined the Olympic movement with digital competitions.

A 100-Year-Old Man Ran a Marathon
Fauja Singh completed one in 8 hours and 11 minutes — proving it's never too late to start running.

Tug-of-War Used to Be an Olympic Sport
Teams of eight pulled on a rope in the Olympics until 1920 — and it might even make a comeback someday.

From billion-dollar stadiums to backyard games, sports show how far people will go for fun, teamwork, and the thrill of competition. Whether it's a moonshot golf ball or a digital victory royale, the spirit of play never gets old.

Basketball Was Invented by a Gym Teacher With a Peach Basket.

Chapter 15: Fashion & Style

Fashion isn't just about clothes — it's about expression, rebellion, and creativity. From sneakers worth millions to hairstyles that caused revolutions, fashion has always been one of the loudest ways to say, "This is who I am." Get ready for a walk through the weird, the stylish, and the totally unexpected world of fashion.

High Heels Were Originally Worn by Men
In the 1600s, European noblemen wore heels to appear taller and more powerful — especially on horseback.

Blue Jeans Were Invented for Miners
Levi Strauss designed them in the 1870s with metal rivets so gold miners wouldn't rip their pants while working.

Sneakers Got Their Name Because They're Quiet
In the late 1800s, people realized rubber soles made shoes "sneaky," since you couldn't hear someone walking in them.

The World's Longest Fashion Show Lasted 30 Hours
It took place in France and featured over 500 outfits on a single runway.

Crocs Were First Made for Boating
They were designed to prevent slipping on wet surfaces — but somehow became a global fashion icon.

Someone Once Made a Dress Out of Spider Silk
It took over a million spiders and years of weaving to create a golden, shimmering gown now displayed in a museum.

Denim Was Originally from France
The word "denim" comes from "serge de Nîmes," meaning "fabric from Nîmes," the town where it was first made.

Lipstick Used to Be Illegal in England
In the 1700s, women could be accused of witchcraft for wearing lipstick — people believed it had magical powers.

The First Fashion Magazine Was Published in 1672
Called *Le Mercure Galant,* it showed drawings of trendy French outfits for Europe's elite.

T-Shirts Were Once Just Underwear
Before the 1950s, no one wore them in public — until movie stars like James Dean made them cool.

There's a "Shoe Museum" in Toronto
It houses over 13,000 pairs of shoes, including ones worn by Queen Victoria and Marilyn Monroe.

People Used to Powder Their Hair Blue
In the 1700s, wealthy Europeans used colored powder made from starch and perfume to style their hair.

The Most Expensive Dress Ever Sold Cost Over $5 Million
Marilyn Monroe's sparkly gown from when she sang "Happy Birthday" to President Kennedy broke all auction records.

Sunglasses Were First Worn by Judges
In ancient China, judges used smoky quartz lenses to hide their facial expressions during trials.

The First Pair of Nike Shoes Was Made in a Waffle Iron
Co-founder Bill Bowerman used his wife's waffle maker to create the shoe's unique grippy sole.

The Hoodie Was Invented for Factory Workers
In the 1930s, it helped warehouse workers stay warm — decades before it became streetwear.

Ancient Egyptians Invented Eye Makeup
They used crushed minerals like malachite and charcoal to protect their eyes from the sun and infections.

Pockets Were Originally Only Sewn Into Men's Clothes
Women had to wear small tied-on bags under their dresses until the 1900s, when pockets finally became common.

A Pair of Air Jordans Once Sold for $2.2 Million
They were game-worn by Michael Jordan himself — making them the most expensive sneakers ever sold.

Lady Gaga Wore a Dress Made of Raw Meat
At the 2010 MTV Awards, she wore a gown made entirely from steak to make a statement about individuality.

Platform Shoes Have Existed for Thousands of Years
Even ancient Greeks wore thick-soled sandals to stay above mud and dirt in theaters.

The Color Pink Used to Be for Boys
In the early 1900s, pink was considered bold and masculine — blue was seen as soft and feminine.

Velcro Was Inspired by a Dog's Fur
A Swiss engineer invented it after noticing how burrs stuck to his dog's coat after a hike.

Fashion Week Happens All Over the World
Major shows take place in Paris, Milan, New York, and Tokyo — sometimes with designers showing collections months in advance.

The Longest Wedding Veil Was Over 20,000 Feet Long
It was worn by a bride in Cyprus and was longer than 60 football fields combined.

In the Middle Ages, Purple Was Reserved for Royalty
The dye came from rare sea snails, making it more expensive than gold.

Some Jeans Are Designed to Fade in Patterns
Brands use lasers or sandblasting to give denim that "perfectly worn" look without years of use.

Perfume Was Invented to Mask Bad Smells
Before daily showers existed, people used scented oils and sprays to stay "fresh."

Fashion always finds a way to reinvent itself — from royal robes to recycled sneakers. Whether it's ancient eyeliner or futuristic fabrics, style is one thing that never goes out of fashion: being yourself.

Perfume Was Invented to Mask Bad Smells.

Chapter 16: Art & Creativity

Art isn't just about painting on a canvas — it's about ideas, emotions, and sometimes total chaos. From melted clocks to invisible sculptures, the art world is full of surprises that make people ask, "Wait... is that *really* art?" Creativity has no limits, and that's what makes it so endlessly fascinating.

The World's Most Expensive Painting Sold for $450 Million
Leonardo da Vinci's *Salvator Mundi* became the priciest artwork ever sold — and some experts still argue if it's 100% his.

A Banana Duct-Taped to a Wall Sold for $120,000
At an art show in Miami, a real banana taped to a wall was sold as "conceptual art." The artist said it represented "commerce itself."

Picasso Could Draw Before He Could Walk
By age nine, Pablo Picasso was already painting masterpieces — his first word was reportedly "piz," short for *lápiz*, meaning "pencil."

Van Gogh Only Sold One Painting While He Was Alive
He sold *The Red Vineyard* for a small sum — but today, his art is worth hundreds of millions.

There's an Entire Museum Dedicated to Bad Art
The Museum of Bad Art in Massachusetts collects paintings so hilariously awful that they become masterpieces of failure.

Banksy Once Shredded His Own Artwork After It Sold
Right after one of his paintings was auctioned for over a million dollars, it self-destructed through a hidden shredder inside the frame.

The Mona Lisa Has No Eyebrows
Historians think they faded or were removed during a restoration — or that da Vinci just never finished them.

An Artist Once Sold "Invisible Sculptures" for Thousands
Italian artist Salvatore Garau sold air — claiming the buyer was purchasing an "idea." The sculpture didn't physically exist.

Crayola Has Retired Over 50 Colors
Some crayons, like "Blizzard Blue" and "Magic Mint," have been discontinued to make room for new shades.

An Elephant Once Painted a Self-Portrait
A Thai elephant named Suda learned to hold a brush and paint herself with stunning accuracy.

Michelangelo Didn't Want to Paint the Sistine Chapel
He saw himself as a sculptor, not a painter, and called the project "a punishment." It still became one of the most famous works ever.

A Street Artist Once Drew With Dirt Instead of Paint
Artist Scott Wade makes temporary car window art using dust — until the rain washes it all away.

The World's Largest Drawing Covers Over 6,000 Feet
It was created in Dubai by a 9-year-old boy using only crayons and pure determination.

A Painting Once Hid Another Painting Beneath It
Using X-ray technology, experts discovered a hidden portrait under Picasso's *The Blue Room*.

The Starry Night Was Painted in an Asylum
Van Gogh painted his most famous piece while recovering in a mental hospital in France.

Lego Is Considered an Official Art Medium
Artists and museums now use Lego bricks to build massive sculptures worth thousands of dollars.

Salvador Dalí Once Showed Up to a Lecture in a Diving Suit
He wore the suit to symbolize how deeply he was "diving into the human mind." He nearly suffocated before removing it.

The World's Largest Sculpture Is Still Being Built
The Crazy Horse Memorial in South Dakota will be over 560 feet tall — even bigger than Mount Rushmore.

Bob Ross Completed Almost Every Painting in 30 Minutes
He filmed *The Joy of Painting* in real-time, creating a finished landscape in every episode.

An Artist Used Melted Chocolate Instead of Paint
Vik Muniz created portraits using edible materials like syrup, peanut butter, and yes — actual chocolate.

Some Museums Hire "Smell Curators"
These experts recreate historical scents — like the smell of ancient temples or an old artist's studio.

There's a Type of Art You Can Only See Under UV Light
Fluorescent paints reveal hidden designs when hit with blacklight, turning ordinary art into glowing masterpieces.

Someone Once Traded a Drawing for a Hotel Stay — Forever
In 1912, artist Al Hirschfeld paid for a New York hotel room with a sketch. The hotel honored the deal for decades.

A Painting in a Museum Once "Ate" a Visitor's Wallet
A modern art sculpture designed to "consume" small objects accidentally shredded a tourist's wallet after he dropped it inside.

Coloring Books for Adults Became a Global Trend
They're now used as stress relief, proving that creativity doesn't stop at childhood.

Some Artists Paint With Coffee or Wine
Instead of traditional paint, they use natural stains to create portraits and landscapes that smell amazing.

From crayons to creativity made of thin air, art proves that imagination has no rules. Whether it's a banana on a wall or a masterpiece in a museum, what matters most is the story it tells — and how it makes you feel.

An Elephant Once Painted a Self-Portrait.

Chapter 17: School & Learning Oddities

School isn't just about homework and tests — it's full of wild traditions, weird rules, and unexpected inventions. From classrooms in caves to pencils that can write in space, learning has a much stranger history than most people realize. Get ready to see education from a whole new angle!

There's a School Built Inside a Cave in China
A remote mountain community created a classroom inside a natural cave because it was the only shelter large enough to fit everyone.

Finland Has Almost No Homework
Students there spend less time studying but score among the highest in the world — proving that balance can beat burnout.

Pencils Can Write in Space — Without Ink
NASA developed mechanical pencils and special pens that work in zero gravity so astronauts could take notes in orbit.

A Student Invented Earmuffs
In 1873, a 15-year-old named Chester Greenwood came up with earmuffs to keep his ears warm while ice skating — and patented them.

The World's Largest School Has Over 50,000 Students
City Montessori School in India holds the record, with tens of thousands of kids studying under one giant system.

Some Japanese Schools Don't Hire Janitors
Students clean their classrooms and hallways themselves to teach responsibility and respect for shared spaces.

There's a School That Floats on Water
In flood-prone areas of Bangladesh, floating schools use solar panels and boats so students can keep learning even during monsoon season.

Einstein Failed His First Entrance Exam
When applying to a Swiss school, young Albert Einstein didn't pass the language and history sections — though he aced math and science.

A Teacher Once Taught an Entire Class Using TikTok
During lockdown, one teacher made short, funny lessons that went viral — proving that learning can happen anywhere.

The World's Oldest University Is Over 1,000 Years Old
The University of al-Qarawiyyin in Morocco was founded in 859 CE by a woman named Fatima al-Fihri.

Some Schools Have "Nap Time" for Teens
In China and Japan, certain high schools allow short naps after lunch to boost focus and energy.

In South Korea, Students Study Until Midnight
High schoolers often stay at special night schools called *hagwons* to prepare for college entrance exams.

There's a School That Teaches Only Wizardry
Yes, really — the "Real-Life School of Witchcraft and Wizardry" in the UK offers classes on potion-making and magical history (for fun).

Teachers Used to Write With Goose Feathers
Before pencils and pens, quills dipped in ink were the main tool for writing essays and taking notes.

In Ancient Greece, Students Wrote on Wax Tablets
They used wooden frames filled with wax and wrote on them with metal styluses that could be erased with heat.

The World's Shortest School Bus Ride Lasted 12 Seconds
A student in Alaska lived so close to school that the bus trip covered less than 500 feet.

Some Schools Have Vending Machines for Books
In New York and Los Angeles, book vending machines let students "buy" books for free using tokens for good behavior.

Finland Once Tried "Outdoor Classrooms" Year-Round
Even in winter, students attended lessons outside to enjoy fresh air — bundled up in snow suits and gloves.

The Bell System in Schools Was Inspired by Factories
The idea of ringing bells to mark time came from the Industrial Revolution, where workers followed timed shifts.

A School Principal Once Slept on the Roof to Motivate Students
To encourage kids to read more books, an Ohio principal promised to camp out on the school roof if they hit their goal — and he did!

There's a High School Inside a Shopping Mall
In the Philippines, a public high school was built inside a mall to make use of empty commercial space.

You Can Major in "Meme Studies"
Some universities now offer pop culture classes focused entirely on internet memes and their social impact.

In Some Countries, Students Sing to Start the Day
In Japan, schools often begin with a song to build community and enthusiasm before classes begin.

A Teacher in France Taught an Entire Lesson in VR
Using virtual reality headsets, students explored ancient Rome in 3D without leaving their classroom.

There's a School With No Grades or Tests
In California, the "Sudbury Model" school lets students choose what to study and how they learn — no exams required.

Some Teachers Grade Homework With Stickers, Not Red Pens
Studies show positive feedback motivates students more than traditional marks — and who doesn't love stickers?

The Word "School" Comes From a Greek Word Meaning "Leisure"
Originally, "scholē" meant free time for thinking and learning — not endless assignments!

The World Record for Longest Class Ever Is 111 Hours
A teacher in India lectured for nearly five days straight to raise awareness about education.

From classrooms in caves to lessons in virtual reality, school is constantly evolving — and it's way weirder than you'd think. Learning doesn't have to happen in a classroom — sometimes the best lessons are the ones that surprise you.

There's a School Built Inside a Cave in China.

Chapter 18: Everyday Objects

We use thousands of everyday things without ever thinking about where they came from — or how strange their stories really are. From the accidental creation of Play-Doh to why your keyboard isn't in alphabetical order, the world around us is full of surprises hiding in plain sight. Let's uncover the wild history behind ordinary stuff!

Bubble Wrap Was Invented as Wallpaper
Two engineers tried to make textured wallpaper in the 1950s. It flopped as home décor — but became perfect for protecting packages instead.

Play-Doh Was Originally a Wallpaper Cleaner
Before becoming a kids' toy, Play-Doh was used to clean soot from walls. When kids started playing with it, the company rebranded it as a toy.

Post-it Notes Were Created by Accident
A scientist at 3M was trying to make a super-strong glue — instead, he made a super-weak one that turned out to be perfect for sticky notes.

Toothpaste Used to Be Made of Crushed Shells
Ancient Egyptians cleaned their teeth with a gritty mix of burnt eggshells, pumice, and ashes long before minty toothpaste existed.

The First Alarm Clocks Could Only Ring Once a Day
Invented in the 1780s, they had to be manually set and couldn't reset themselves — so if you missed it, tough luck!

Q-Tips Were Inspired by a Father's Observation
Leo Gerstenzang invented them after seeing his wife use cotton on a toothpick to clean their baby's ears.

The Eraser Was Invented by Mistake
Before rubber, people used bread crumbs to erase pencil marks. Then someone accidentally grabbed a piece of rubber — and realized it worked better.

Velcro Came From a Hike With a Dog
A Swiss engineer noticed burrs sticking to his dog's fur and recreated the idea with tiny hooks and loops — calling it "Velcro."

Your Keyboard Isn't Alphabetical on Purpose
The QWERTY layout was designed to slow typists down so old typewriters wouldn't jam.

The Microwave Was Invented by Accident
An engineer noticed a candy bar melting in his pocket while working with radar waves — and that's how microwave ovens were born.

The First Credit Card Was Made for a Forgotten Wallet
A man created "Diners Club" after being embarrassed for not having cash at a restaurant. It became the world's first charge card.

Toilet Paper Was a Luxury Item
In the 1800s, it was sold in fancy boxes, and only rich families could afford it. Most people used newspapers or leaves instead.

The Shopping Cart Wasn't Popular at First
When it debuted in 1937, people refused to use it — until stores hired actors to casually push them around and make them look cool.

Pens Have Tiny Holes to Prevent Explosions
That little hole in your pen cap? It equalizes air pressure so ink doesn't leak — or worse, burst mid-flight.

Zippers Were Once Called "Automatic Continuous Clothing Closures"
The name didn't catch on (obviously). "Zipper" came later, thanks to the sound it makes.

Bubble Gum Was Invented by a Bookkeeper
In 1928, Walter Diemer mixed up a new kind of chewing gum at work — and it turned out to be the first that could blow bubbles.

The First Pair of Sunglasses Was for Judges
In ancient China, smoky quartz lenses helped judges hide their expressions during court cases.

The Color of Erasers Has a Reason
Pink erasers were made from pumice and red dye — materials that just happened to be available together.

Jeans Were Designed for Gold Miners
Levi Strauss created denim pants with metal rivets so miners wouldn't rip them while working.

The First Frisbee Was a Pie Tin
College students started tossing empty tins from the Frisbie Pie Company — which inspired the modern flying disc.

Paper Clips Were Used as a Symbol of Resistance
During World War II, Norwegians wore paper clips on their lapels to silently protest Nazi occupation.

The First Cell Phones Weighed Two Pounds
The Motorola DynaTAC, released in 1983, was so heavy and bulky it was nicknamed "the brick."

Straws Used to Be Made of Rye Grass
Before paper or plastic, people sipped through hollow stems — but they added a grassy taste to drinks.

The Ballpoint Pen Solved a Big Messy Problem
Invented in the 1930s, it replaced messy fountain pens that leaked ink everywhere.

The First Remote Control Was Connected by a Wire
Before wireless remotes, early TV remotes had long cords — so people kept tripping over them.

Sticky Tape Was Invented During the Great Depression
Scotch tape was created to help people repair instead of replace things when money was tight.

Your Sneakers' Rubber Soles Were Inspired by Car Tires
Manufacturers used vulcanized rubber — the same tough, flexible material used for tires — to make durable soles.

Scissors Are Over 3,000 Years Old
Ancient Egyptians used bronze scissors that looked almost identical to modern ones.

The Small Hole in Airplane Windows Keeps You Safe
It balances air pressure so the glass doesn't crack during flight.

Every object around you has a hidden story — a mix of creativity, accidents, and clever problem-solving. Next time you pick up a pen, zip your hoodie, or unwrap gum, remember: even ordinary things started with one extraordinary idea.

The First Remote Control Was Connected by a Wire.

Chapter 19: Weather & Natural Disasters

Weather can be beautiful, terrifying, and completely unpredictable. From rains of fish to lightning that never stops, nature constantly reminds us how powerful it really is. These facts show the strange, wild, and mind-blowing sides of the forces shaping our planet every day.

It Can Actually Rain Fish
In a small town in Honduras, fish fall from the sky every year during a storm known as "Lluvia de Peces." Scientists think strong winds lift them from nearby rivers.

Lightning Can Strike the Same Place Twice
The Empire State Building in New York gets hit by lightning about 25 times every year! Tall structures attract electricity more often than open fields.

There's a Place Where It Never Stops Lightning
Lake Maracaibo in Venezuela experiences lightning storms almost every single night — up to 260 days a year.

Snow Can Be Pink or Red
In cold climates, certain algae grow on snow, giving it a red or pink tint known as "watermelon snow."

The Strongest Wind Ever Recorded Reached 254 mph
During a tropical cyclone in Australia, wind speeds were so extreme that meteorologists had trouble keeping their instruments from breaking.

Tornadoes Can Toss Cars Like Toys
The most powerful tornadoes, called EF5s, can lift entire vehicles and hurl them over 100 yards away.

Rainbows Can Be Full Circles
From an airplane, you can sometimes see a complete circle instead of the half-arc we usually spot from the ground.

There's a Fire Tornado Called a "Firenado"
When wildfires meet strong winds, spinning columns of flames can form — they look unreal but are completely natural.

The Coldest Temperature on Earth Was -144°F
In Antarctica, scientists recorded this freezing low using satellite data — it's so cold that even breathing can be dangerous.

Hailstones Can Be the Size of Softballs
The largest hailstone ever recorded in the U.S. weighed nearly two pounds and was found in South Dakota.

A Thunderstorm Once Produced 200,000 Lightning Bolts
This record-setting storm hit France in 2022, with lightning flashing for over eight hours straight.

It Once Rained for Two Years Straight
In one region of India, a constant drizzle lasted from 1860 to 1862 — locals said it never stopped long enough to dry anything.

Earthquakes Can Make Rivers Flow Backward
During powerful quakes, the ground's shaking can reverse river currents for a short time — it's happened along the Mississippi River.

Volcanoes Can Create Their Own Weather
Explosive eruptions shoot ash and steam high enough to generate lightning storms inside volcanic clouds.

You Can Smell Rain Before It Arrives
That fresh, earthy scent is called "petrichor" — it's caused by oils from plants mixing with chemicals released by raindrops hitting the ground.

Sandstorms Can Travel Across Oceans
Dust from the Sahara Desert has been tracked flying all the way to South America — over 3,000 miles away.

There's a River of Clouds in the Sky
Called "atmospheric rivers," these massive streams of water vapor carry more moisture than the Amazon River itself.

Hurricanes Rotate in Different Directions Depending on Where You Are
In the Northern Hemisphere, they spin counterclockwise — in the Southern Hemisphere, it's the opposite.

Lightning Can Be Hotter Than the Sun
A single lightning bolt can reach 50,000°F — five times hotter than the surface of the sun.

The Dead Sea Is Slowly Shrinking
Because it's evaporating faster than it's being refilled, this famously salty lake loses about three feet of water each year.

Tsunamis Can Move Faster Than a Jet Plane
Some travel at speeds up to 500 mph — and can cross entire oceans in just a few hours.

The Sahara Desert Used to Be Green
Thousands of years ago, it was covered in grasslands and rivers before climate shifts turned it into the world's biggest desert.

There's a City That Gets 400 Inches of Snow Every Year
Aomori, Japan, is one of the snowiest places on Earth — cars there often disappear completely under snowdrifts.

The Eye of a Hurricane Can Be Peaceful
Inside the storm's center, winds die down, and the sky can even turn clear — but only for a short time before chaos returns.

A Volcano Once Erupted So Loudly It Was Heard 3,000 Miles Away
When Krakatoa exploded in 1883, the sound was heard as far as Australia — the loudest noise in recorded history.

Earthquakes Can Trigger Hundreds of Aftershocks
One major quake can cause smaller tremors for days or even months afterward as the ground settles again.

Some Tornadoes Are Invisible
If they don't pick up dirt or debris, you might not see them — just the swirling air and destruction they leave behind.

The Hottest Temperature Ever Recorded Was 134°F
It happened in Death Valley, California, where the heat is so extreme that tires can melt on the asphalt.

From raining fish to lightning storms that never end, Earth's weather proves it's one of the most powerful and unpredictable forces in the universe. Every gust, flash, and raindrop reminds us just how wild our planet really is.

It Can Actually Rain Fish.

Chapter 20: The Ocean & Underwater World

The ocean covers more than 70% of our planet, but humans have explored less than 10% of it. It's home to glowing creatures, hidden mountains, and animals so weird they look like aliens. Dive in — these underwater facts will make you see the sea in a whole new way!

There's an Entire Mountain Range Under the Ocean
The Mid-Atlantic Ridge is the world's longest mountain chain — and it's completely underwater, stretching over 40,000 miles.

Some Fish Can Walk on Land
The mudskipper uses its fins to crawl along beaches and even climb rocks when the tide goes out.

The Deepest Point on Earth Is Deeper Than Mount Everest Is Tall
The Mariana Trench plunges nearly 36,000 feet — if you dropped Everest into it, the peak would still be underwater.

There Are Lakes and Rivers Under the Sea
In some places, super-salty water forms underwater "pools" that look just like lakes — complete with waves and shorelines.

The Ocean Glows at Night in Some Places
Bioluminescent plankton light up when the water moves, creating glowing blue waves that look straight out of a movie.

Sharks Were Around Before Trees Existed
Sharks have been swimming in Earth's oceans for more than 400 million years — way before forests appeared.

The Ocean Has Its Own Internet
Thousands of miles of fiber-optic cables run along the sea floor, carrying most of the world's internet traffic.

Whale Songs Can Travel for Thousands of Miles
Blue whales use low-frequency sounds that can be heard across entire oceans by other whales.

Some Jellyfish Can Live Forever
The *Turritopsis dohrnii* jellyfish can revert its cells back to a younger stage, basically resetting its life cycle.

There's an Entire Waterfall Under the Ocean
Between Greenland and Iceland, cold dense water flows under warmer water, forming the largest "underwater waterfall" on Earth.

An Octopus Has a Brain in Each Arm
Each of its eight arms can think and act independently, making it one of the smartest sea creatures alive.

The Deep Ocean Is Pitch Black and Freezing Cold
Sunlight only reaches about 3% of the ocean's depth — below that, it's total darkness and near-freezing temperatures.

Seahorses Are the Only Animals Where Males Give Birth
Male seahorses carry babies in a special pouch until they're ready to swim away.

There's Gold in the Ocean
The seas contain around 20 million tons of dissolved gold — but it's spread too thin to mine profitably.

Some Crabs Wear Living "Hats"
Decorator crabs attach seaweed, shells, and even sponges to their shells for camouflage and protection.

The Loudest Sound Ever Recorded Came From an Ocean
"The Bloop," a mysterious underwater noise recorded in 1997, was louder than any known whale — later discovered to be caused by cracking icebergs.

The Ocean Has Its Own Seasons
Just like land, water temperatures and currents shift throughout the year, changing marine life patterns and migration routes.

A Giant Squid's Eyes Are the Size of Dinner Plates
Their massive eyes help them spot predators, like sperm whales, in the dark deep sea.

Coral Is Actually Alive
What looks like colorful rock is a colony of tiny animals called polyps — and coral reefs are some of the most diverse ecosystems on Earth.

Sea Cucumbers Breathe Through Their Butts
It sounds like a joke, but they really absorb oxygen through their rear end — it's a built-in life support system!

The Ocean Has Underwater Volcanoes That Erupt Constantly
More volcanic activity happens on the seafloor than on land, creating new crust and islands over time.

Some Fish Can Change Gender
Clownfish and wrasses can switch from male to female (or vice versa) depending on their environment or social group.

The Great Barrier Reef Is Visible From Space
It's the largest living structure on Earth, stretching more than 1,400 miles along Australia's coast.

There Are "Zombie Worms" That Eat Bones
These deep-sea worms feast on the skeletons of whales that fall to the ocean floor.

The Deepest-Diving Mammal Is the Cuvier's Beaked Whale
It can dive more than 10,000 feet deep and stay underwater for over two hours.

A Blobfish Looks Totally Normal in Its Natural Habitat
It only looks "melty" when brought to the surface because the pressure difference causes its body to expand.

Giant Kelp Can Grow Two Feet a Day
This ocean plant grows faster than almost any other organism on Earth, forming massive underwater forests.

The Ocean Is Slowly Getting Louder
Ship engines, sonar, and underwater drilling create "noise pollution" that can confuse whales and dolphins.

The ocean is like another world — full of glowing, shape-shifting, and mind-bending creatures. We've explored more of space than the deep sea, which means there are still thousands of mysteries waiting below the waves.

The Ocean Has Underwater Volcanoes That Erupt Constantly.

Chapter 21: Space Exploration & NASA

From the first moon landing to exploring distant planets, space exploration has pushed the limits of human imagination and technology. NASA's missions have revealed breathtaking worlds, daring astronauts, and some hilarious space surprises. Get ready to blast off into some of the most fascinating facts about humanity's adventures beyond Earth!

Astronauts Grow Taller in Space
Without gravity compressing their spines, astronauts can stretch up to two inches taller while in orbit — though they shrink back on Earth.

Space Smells Like Burnt Steak
Astronauts describe the scent that clings to their suits after a spacewalk as metallic and smoky — kind of like seared steak or gunpowder.

Neil Armstrong's Footprints Are Still on the Moon
With no wind or rain on the Moon, the footprints from the Apollo 11 mission could stay visible for millions of years.

NASA Once Accidentally Erased the Original Moon Landing Tapes
In the 1980s, NASA reused the tapes from the Apollo 11 mission — losing the original high-quality footage forever.

Space Isn't Completely Silent
While sound can't travel through a vacuum, electromagnetic waves from stars and planets can be converted into eerie space "music."

The First Food Eaten on the Moon Was Bacon
NASA packed special bacon cubes for the Apollo 11 astronauts — because even in space, breakfast is important.

NASA's First Computer Was the Size of a Room
The Apollo Guidance Computer was revolutionary for its time but had less processing power than a modern calculator.

Astronauts Can't Burp in Space
Without gravity, gas and liquids mix in the stomach — so burping would cause… other problems.

There's a "Space Cemetery" in the Pacific Ocean
Decommissioned satellites and spacecraft are steered to crash in a remote area called Point Nemo — the farthest spot from any land.

The Moon Has Moonquakes
Just like Earth has earthquakes, the Moon shakes too! NASA instruments recorded "moonquakes" caused by tidal stress and meteor impacts.

NASA Once Sent a Piece of a Wright Brothers Plane to Mars
A small piece of the original 1903 Wright Flyer was attached to the Ingenuity helicopter that flew on Mars in 2021.

The International Space Station Travels at 17,500 mph
That means astronauts circle Earth about every 90 minutes — watching 16 sunrises and sunsets a day.

NASA Uses Scented Training Rooms for Space Missions
They recreate smells like metal, burnt rubber, and body odor to prepare astronauts for life inside a spacecraft.

Spacesuits Cost More Than a Mansion
Each modern NASA spacesuit costs about $12 million — most of it for the life-support systems inside.

There's Wi-Fi on the Space Station
Astronauts can browse the internet, send emails, and even post on social media while orbiting Earth.

NASA Plants Trees for Every Astronaut
Since the 1960s, NASA has planted a tree for every astronaut who has flown to space — it's called the "Astronaut Grove."

One NASA Engineer Invented the Super Soaker
Lonnie Johnson, a NASA scientist, was testing a heat pump when he accidentally created the world's most famous water gun.

The First Woman in Space Was From the Soviet Union
Valentina Tereshkova orbited Earth 48 times in 1963 — years before the U.S. sent its first female astronaut.

NASA Once Sent Music to Space
The Voyager probes each carry a "Golden Record" with music, greetings, and sounds from Earth — just in case aliens find it.

Astronauts' Tears Don't Fall Down
Without gravity, tears stick to their eyes and form floating blobs of water instead of rolling down their cheeks.

NASA's Logo Is Nicknamed "The Meatball"
The round blue logo with stars and a red swoosh got its nickname from employees who thought it looked tasty.

Space Toilets Use Air Instead of Water
Since water doesn't flow in zero gravity, suction systems use air to pull waste away — very carefully.

There's a Hidden Message on the Mars Rover's Parachute
When Perseverance landed in 2021, its parachute's pattern secretly spelled "Dare Mighty Things" in binary code.

NASA Once Sent Astronauts to Live in an Underwater Base
They trained in an underwater habitat called Aquarius to simulate the isolation and pressure of long space missions.

The Coldest Spot in the Universe Was Created by NASA
Scientists on the ISS cooled atoms to nearly absolute zero to study quantum physics — colder than deep space itself.

Astronauts Use Velcro for Everything
In zero gravity, they stick pens, tools, and even food packets to Velcro so nothing floats away.

NASA Has a Planetary Protection Officer
Their job is to prevent contamination — making sure we don't bring germs to other planets or back from them.

Mars Rovers Sing Themselves "Happy Birthday"
NASA programmed the Curiosity rover to play "Happy Birthday" using its sample-analysis instruments each year on August 5.

The Voyager 1 Probe Is Still Sending Signals — From 15 Billion Miles Away
Launched in 1977, it's the farthest human-made object from Earth and still communicates with NASA today.

From moon landings to Mars rovers, every NASA mission is a mix of science, bravery, and imagination. The sky isn't the limit — it's just the beginning of where human curiosity can take us.

Neil Armstrong's Footprints Are Still on the Moon.

Chapter 22: Ancient Civilizations

Long before smartphones and skyscrapers, ancient civilizations built incredible cities, invented amazing technologies, and left behind mysteries we still can't explain. From underwater ruins to secret writing systems, these ancient people were way ahead of their time. Let's explore the secrets they left buried in stone, sand, and legend.

The Ancient Egyptians Had Prosthetic Toes
Archaeologists found a 3,000-year-old wooden big toe on a mummy — one of the world's earliest prosthetics, proving Egyptians cared about both function and fashion.

The Mayans Invented a Ball Game That Could End in Sacrifice
Their sport, called *pok-ta-pok*, involved hitting a rubber ball through a stone hoop without using hands or feet — and losing could be deadly.

The Romans Built Roads So Well They're Still Used Today
Some Roman roads are over 2,000 years old and still form the foundation for modern European highways.

Ancient Chinese Engineers Built the First Seismograph
Over 1,800 years ago, Zhang Heng invented a device that could detect earthquakes hundreds of miles away — using bronze dragons that dropped metal balls when the earth shook.

The Vikings Wore Eye Makeup
Despite their tough image, both Viking men and women used black eyeliner made from crushed minerals — not for vanity, but to protect their eyes from the sun's glare.

There's a City Hidden Beneath the Pyramids
Archaeologists have found tunnels and chambers under Egypt's pyramids that might have been used for rituals or hidden treasures.

Ancient Greeks Used Vending Machines
Invented by Hero of Alexandria, the machine dispensed holy water when a coin was dropped in — proving convenience is not a modern idea.

The Aztecs Used Chocolate as Money
Cocoa beans were so valuable that people used them as currency to buy food, clothes, and even pay taxes.

Cleopatra Lived Closer to the Moon Landing Than to the Building of the Pyramids
The Great Pyramid was already 2,000 years old when Cleopatra ruled Egypt — ancient history was ancient even for the ancients.

The Incas Built Cities Without Cement
Their stone walls fit together so precisely that not even a knife blade can fit between the blocks — and they've survived massive earthquakes.

There's an Ancient "Computer" From 100 BC
The Antikythera Mechanism, found in a shipwreck, could predict eclipses and track planets — it's often called the world's first analog computer.

Ancient Egyptians Used Honey as Medicine
They treated wounds with honey because it kills bacteria — modern science has proven they were absolutely right.

The Greeks Had Automatic Doors
In temples, they used steam power to open massive bronze doors — a technology lost for centuries afterward.

The City of Pompeii Was Preserved by a Volcano
When Mount Vesuvius erupted in 79 AD, it buried Pompeii in ash so perfectly that archaeologists can still see people's final moments.

Ancient Persians Invented Air Conditioning
They built wind towers that cooled buildings by channeling breezes underground — centuries before electricity existed.

Stonehenge Was Built Before the Pyramids
The massive stone circle in England is older than Egypt's pyramids by nearly 500 years — and we still don't know exactly how it was built.

The First Brain Surgery Dates Back 7,000 Years
Prehistoric skulls show signs of trepanation — holes cut into the head, sometimes with the patients surviving the procedure.

The Great Library of Alexandria Held Over 500,000 Scrolls
It was the most advanced knowledge hub of the ancient world — and its mysterious destruction erased centuries of wisdom.

Ancient Romans Had Heated Floors
Their "hypocaust" systems used furnaces beneath floors to warm rooms — luxury living, ancient-style.

A Lost City Was Found Under the Jungle
Using laser technology, researchers discovered vast Mayan cities hidden beneath the Guatemalan rainforest, complete with highways and temples.

Ancient Egyptians Used Toothpaste
Their recipe included mint, rock salt, and pepper — not exactly minty fresh, but surprisingly effective.

The Greek Fire Weapon Was a Secret for Centuries
It was a burning liquid used in naval battles that could set even water on fire — and no one ever discovered the exact formula.

Some Ancient Statues Were Painted, Not White
Greek and Roman statues we see as marble-white today were once brightly colored — time just stripped away the paint.

The Olmecs Carved Giant Stone Heads Without Metal Tools
Each head weighs up to 40 tons, and no one knows exactly how they moved them through dense jungles.

There's a Pyramid Older Than Egypt's — in Sudan
The ancient Kingdom of Kush built more pyramids than Egypt, many smaller but beautifully preserved.

The First Recorded Joke Comes From Ancient Sumer
It's over 4,000 years old and about... gas. Yep — toilet humor is truly timeless.

The Romans Used Concrete That Gets Stronger Over Time
Modern scientists discovered volcanic ash helped their concrete heal itself when cracks formed — something we're only now trying to recreate.

Ancient Japan Had "Nail-Free" Temples
Builders used wooden joints and clever engineering to create massive temples without a single metal nail.

Atlantis Might Have Been Real
Some historians think the legend of Atlantis could have been inspired by the ancient island of Santorini, which was destroyed by a massive volcanic eruption.

From hidden cities to mind-blowing inventions, ancient civilizations prove that humans have always been creative, curious, and full of surprises. The past may be old, but it's never boring — and we're still uncovering its secrets every day.

A Lost City Was Found Under the Jungle.

Chapter 23: Tiny vs. Giant

From the tiniest living creatures to the biggest structures ever built, our world is full of jaw-dropping size extremes. Some things are so small they fit inside a cell, while others are so massive they can be seen from space. Get ready to zoom in and out of the most mind-blowing examples of "tiny vs. giant" the world has to offer!

The Smallest Mammal Could Fit on Your Thumb
The bumblebee bat of Thailand weighs less than a penny and is about the size of a large bumblebee.

The Blue Whale's Heart Is the Size of a Car
A blue whale's heart can weigh over 400 pounds — and its heartbeat can be detected from two miles away.

Ants Never Sleep
Instead of resting like humans, ants take short "power pauses" throughout the day while continuing to work.

Mount Everest Can Grow Taller
Earthquakes and tectonic movement slowly push Everest upward by about a quarter inch each year.

The World's Smallest Robot Is Thinner Than a Hair
Scientists built a microscopic robot smaller than a grain of salt that can swim through liquid and deliver medicine inside the body.

The Largest Flower Smells Like Rotting Meat
The Rafflesia arnoldii, found in Indonesia, can reach three feet across — and it stinks like death to attract flies.

Your DNA Could Stretch From Earth to the Sun and Back
If you unraveled all the DNA in your body's cells, it would stretch about 600 times from Earth to the Sun.

The World's Biggest Cave Has Its Own Weather
Vietnam's Son Doong Cave is so huge it contains a jungle, clouds, and even a river inside.

A Single Teaspoon of a Neutron Star Weighs as Much as a Mountain
These collapsed stars are so dense that just a spoonful of their material would weigh billions of tons.

Some Spiders Are So Tiny They Can Stand on a Grain of Salt
The Patu digua spider from Colombia measures only 0.015 inches long — barely visible to the human eye.

The Largest Living Organism Covers More Than 2,000 Acres
It's not a whale or a tree — it's a fungus in Oregon called the "Humongous Fungus," and it's over 2,000 years old.

The Smallest Computer Is Smaller Than a Rice Grain
IBM created a working computer so tiny it could sit comfortably on a grain of rice and still process data.

The Tallest Statue in the World Is Twice the Height of the Statue of Liberty
India's "Statue of Unity" stands 597 feet tall — nearly the size of a 60-story building.

Some Microbes Can Survive Inside Rocks
Scientists found bacteria living miles below Earth's surface — surviving in complete darkness, heat, and pressure.

The Biggest Snowflake Ever Recorded Was 15 Inches Wide
It fell in Montana in 1887 and was described as "bigger than a dinner plate."

There Are Trees Taller Than the Statue of Liberty
California's coast redwoods can grow over 370 feet tall — and some are older than the Roman Empire.

The Smallest Bird Weighs Less Than a Dime
The bee hummingbird of Cuba measures just two inches long and beats its wings up to 80 times per second.

The Biggest Animal Brain Belongs to a Sperm Whale
It weighs around 20 pounds — five times heavier than a human brain.

The World's Smallest Dog Can Fit in Your Pocket
A Chihuahua named Pearl holds the record at under four inches tall and barely one pound in weight.

The Tallest Building Has Its Own Clouds
The Burj Khalifa in Dubai is so tall that the temperature at its top can be 15°F cooler than at the bottom.

The World's Largest Insect Weighs More Than a Mouse
The giant wētā from New Zealand can reach nearly three ounces — heavier than a sparrow!

Some Plants Grow Faster Than You Can Blink
Certain bamboo species can grow almost three feet in just 24 hours — that's more than an inch every 40 minutes.

A Drop of Water Can Hold Millions of Living Things
Microscopic organisms like bacteria and plankton thrive in just one tiny droplet of pond water.

The Largest Telescope Can See Billions of Light-Years Away
The James Webb Space Telescope can detect light from galaxies formed shortly after the Big Bang.

The Smallest Frog Is Smaller Than a Fingernail
Discovered in Papua New Guinea, it's so tiny that it can sit comfortably on the head of a pin.

There's an Ant Colony Bigger Than a Country
A supercolony of Argentine ants stretches over 3,700 miles across southern Europe — one of the largest animal networks on Earth.

A Blue Whale's Tongue Weighs as Much as an Elephant
Just one tongue can weigh 6,000 pounds — and it's big enough to hold 50 people.

The World's Smallest Lizard Lives on a Dime
Found in the Caribbean, the tiny gecko *Sphaerodactylus ariasae* measures only 0.6 inches long from nose to tail.

The Universe's Largest Known Structure Is a Cosmic "Wall"
The Hercules–Corona Borealis Great Wall spans 10 billion light-years — it's so massive it challenges what we thought possible about the universe.

From microscopic machines to mountains that scrape the sky, the world of "tiny vs. giant" shows that size doesn't define greatness — wonder does. Whether it's the tiniest frog or the biggest whale, every scale tells its own amazing story.

The Smallest Frog Is Smaller Than a Fingernail.

Chapter 24: Time & Speed

Time is one of the strangest things in the universe — we can't see it, touch it, or stop it, yet it controls everything we do. From lightning-fast animals to clocks that run slower in space, time and speed can bend reality in ways that seem impossible. Let's race through some wild facts that will make your head spin — in the best way!

Time Moves Faster on Mountains
Because gravity is weaker at higher altitudes, clocks on mountaintops tick slightly faster than those at sea level.

You're Moving Right Now — Even Sitting Still
Because Earth spins and orbits the Sun, you're actually racing through space at over 67,000 mph.

There's No Such Thing as "Now" in Space
Einstein's theory of relativity says time passes differently depending on your speed — meaning two people can disagree on what "now" is.

The World's Fastest Roller Coaster Hits 149 mph
Located in Abu Dhabi, Formula Rossa accelerates from 0 to 149 mph in just under five seconds — goggles required!

Cheetahs Don't Stay Fast for Long
They can sprint up to 75 mph, but only for about 20 seconds before overheating.

Astronauts Age Slower in Space
Due to time dilation, people on the International Space Station experience time slightly slower than those on Earth — by a few milliseconds!

The Shortest Unit of Time Has a Name
It's called a *zeptosecond* — a trillionth of a billionth of a second, used to measure atomic reactions.

Your Brain Works on a Delay
It takes about 80 milliseconds for your brain to process what your eyes see — so technically, you're always living slightly in the past.

Some Animals Experience Time Differently
Flies and hummingbirds process visual information so fast that the world seems to move in slow motion to them.

Time Zones Were Invented for Trains
Before railroads, every city kept its own local time. Trains made it too confusing, so standardized time zones were created in the 1800s.

A Second Was Originally Measured by the Stars
Before atomic clocks, scientists defined a second as a fraction of Earth's rotation — now it's based on atomic vibrations.

Light Is the Universe's Speed Limit
Nothing can go faster than light — about 186,000 miles per second — no matter how much power or technology you have.

Some Places Have Two New Years
In Thailand, they celebrate both the traditional Buddhist New Year and the international one on January 1.

The Fastest Thing a Human Has Ever Made Is a Spacecraft
NASA's Parker Solar Probe reached 430,000 mph while flying close to the Sun — that's seven times faster than Earth's orbital speed.

Your Heart Beats About 3 Billion Times in a Lifetime
That's if you live around 80 years — each beat marking a tiny tick of your personal clock.

Days Are Getting Longer
Earth's rotation is slowing down by about 1.7 milliseconds every century, thanks to the Moon's gravitational pull.

You Experience Time Faster When You're Happy
Studies show that excitement and joy make your brain process moments more quickly, making time "fly."

Some Turtles Live for Over 180 Years
Compared to humans, certain giant tortoises move and age at a pace that seems frozen in time.

The Fastest Thing in the Human Body Is a Nerve Signal
Messages between your brain and muscles can travel at up to 270 feet per second.

In Antarctica, There's a Day That Lasts Six Months
Because of Earth's tilt, the Sun stays up for half the year — and disappears for the other half.

Running Makes You Travel Through Time (Sort Of)
The faster you move, the slower time passes for you — but you'd need to run near light speed to notice!

A Lightning Bolt Moves Faster Than You Can Blink
It flashes through the sky at 220,000 mph — faster than your brain can register the sight.

There Are Places Where Time Officially Doesn't Exist
At the South Pole, all time zones meet — so technically, you can choose any time zone you want.

The Fastest Elevator in the World Is in China
It travels nearly 47 mph — reaching the 95th floor in under 45 seconds.
Some Stars Spin So Fast They Flatten
Pulsars can rotate hundreds of times per second, making them slightly squashed instead of perfectly round.
The Speed of Sound Changes With Temperature
Sound moves faster in hot air and slower in cold — that's why thunder seems to travel differently on summer and winter nights.
You Can "See" Back in Time When You Look at Stars
Because light takes years to reach us, starlight is a snapshot of the past — you might be seeing a star that no longer exists.

Time and speed shape everything — from how fast we live to how long our planet spins. Whether it's a falcon diving or an astronaut aging in slow motion, every moment is a reminder that the universe is constantly on the move.

You're Moving Right Now — Even Sitting Still.

Chapter 25: Human Emotions & Psychology

Your brain is a fascinating, emotional roller coaster that controls how you feel, think, and react — even when you don't realize it. From why we blush to how music changes our mood, human emotions and psychology reveal just how weirdly wonderful our minds really are. Let's dive into what makes us tick — and sometimes freak out.

You Can Catch Someone's Mood Like a Cold
Emotions are contagious — when you see someone smile or frown, your brain mirrors their expression and mood automatically.

Your Brain Has a "Delete" Button for Memories
When you stop recalling certain experiences, your brain starts pruning those neural connections to make room for new ones.

Crying Actually Makes You Feel Better
Tears release stress hormones, which helps calm your body and improve your mood afterward.

People Smile in the Same Language Everywhere
No matter where you're from, a genuine smile means the same thing — it's one of the few universal human expressions.

Fear Can Make Time Feel Slower
During scary moments, your brain takes in more detail, tricking you into thinking time is moving slower than it really is.

Your Brain Can Trick You Into Feeling Pain That Isn't Real
Phantom limb syndrome makes amputees feel sensations in limbs they no longer have because their brains still "map" them.

You Remember Negative Things More Easily
The human brain evolved to focus on danger, so bad experiences stick longer in your memory than good ones.

Music Changes Your Heartbeat
Your pulse actually speeds up or slows down to match the rhythm of the song you're listening to.

Blushing Is a Built-In Honesty Signal
When you're embarrassed, blood rushes to your face — a physical reaction that shows others you recognize a social mistake.

Your Brain Is More Active When You're Asleep Than Awake
During deep sleep, your brain processes memories, emotions, and even rehearses problem-solving.

You Can't Tickle Yourself
Your brain predicts your own movements, which cancels out the surprise reaction that tickling normally triggers.

People Remember Stories Better Than Facts
Our brains are wired for storytelling — that's why a good story sticks with you longer than a list of data.

We Have a "Sixth Sense" for Emotion
Humans subconsciously pick up on micro-expressions and tone changes that reveal how others are really feeling.

Smells Are Emotional Time Machines
Scents go directly to the brain's emotional center — that's why a random smell can instantly bring back childhood memories.

You're Most Creative When You're Tired
Your brain is less focused late at night, allowing unusual ideas to sneak through and connect in unexpected ways.

Laughter Is a Form of Social Bonding
People are 30 times more likely to laugh in a group than when alone — it's how humans build trust and connection.

Your Brain Loves to Be Right — Even When It's Wrong
Once you believe something, your brain resists new information that challenges it — it's called confirmation bias.

Love Literally Feels Like a Drug
Falling in love releases dopamine, the same "pleasure chemical" triggered by chocolate or winning a prize.

Your Subconscious Decides Before You Do
Studies show your brain makes choices milliseconds before you're consciously aware of them.

Anger Can Make You Feel Stronger
The adrenaline rush that comes with anger temporarily boosts strength and reaction speed — that's your body going into defense mode.

People Can Feel "Alone in a Crowd"
Being surrounded by people doesn't always make you feel connected — loneliness is more about emotional connection than physical presence.

Your Brain Can't Tell the Difference Between Real and Imagined Stress
Whether you're reliving an argument or facing one now, your body reacts the same way with tension and increased heartbeat.

Happiness Peaks at the Same Time of Day for Most People
Research shows most people report feeling happiest around lunchtime — when energy and social interaction peak.

Humans Are Wired to Imitate
When someone yawns, laughs, or crosses their arms, your brain's mirror neurons fire — making you want to do it too.

Smiling Can Trick Your Brain Into Feeling Happy
Even a fake smile releases endorphins and serotonin, giving your brain a mini mood boost.

You're More Likely to Remember the First and Last Thing You Hear
This is called the "serial position effect" — your brain gives priority to beginnings and endings.

Your Brain Can Rewire Itself for Joy
Practicing gratitude or mindfulness strengthens positive neural pathways, helping you naturally feel happier over time.

Our minds are like emotional supercomputers — powerful, unpredictable, and always learning. The more we understand how emotions work, the better we can use them to connect, create, and stay kind to ourselves and others.

People Smile in the Same Language Everywhere.

Chapter 26: Money & Business

Money makes the world go round — but it also makes for some seriously weird stories. From billion-dollar mistakes to people who got rich by total accident, the world of business is full of surprises. Let's explore the strange, funny, and sometimes unbelievable facts about how money works and who ends up with it.

The First Credit Card Was Made for Forgetful Diners
In 1950, a man forgot his wallet at a restaurant — so he invented the Diners Club Card, the world's first credit card.

There's More Monopoly Money Printed Every Year Than Real Cash
Hasbro prints over $30 billion in Monopoly money annually — more than the U.S. Treasury prints in real dollars.

Apple Makes More Money Than Most Countries
Apple's yearly revenue is higher than the GDP of over 150 countries — including New Zealand and Finland.

The World's Richest Man Once Slept on His Office Floor
When Jeff Bezos founded Amazon, he worked from a garage and used doors as desks to save money.

Paper Money Isn't Actually Paper
U.S. dollars are made from 75% cotton and 25% linen, which makes them more durable than regular paper.

Bitcoin Was Once Used to Buy Pizza
In 2010, someone spent 10,000 bitcoins (worth over $600 million today) on two pizzas — now known as the world's most expensive meal.

A Penny Costs More to Make Than It's Worth
It costs the U.S. Mint about 2.1 cents to produce a one-cent coin.

Disney Started with Just a Cartoon Mouse
Walt Disney built a billion-dollar empire from one character — Mickey Mouse, who debuted in 1928.

There's a $100,000 Bill
The U.S. once printed a $100,000 bill featuring Woodrow Wilson — but it was used only for transactions between banks.

Starbucks Spends More on Employee Health Insurance Than on Coffee Beans
The company prioritizes healthcare benefits, making it one of the most expensive perks in the business world.

McDonald's Makes More Money from Real Estate Than Burgers
The company owns the land and buildings for most of its franchises — it's basically a real estate empire in disguise.

There's an ATM in Antarctica
It's located at a U.S. research base, and it's one of the most remote cash machines on Earth.

Fortune Cookies Aren't From China
They were invented in California — and they're almost unheard of in China itself.

Nike's Logo Cost $35
A design student created the famous swoosh in 1971 and was paid only $35. Later, Nike gave her stock worth millions.

The World's Youngest Billionaire Was Just 19
Alexandr Wang co-founded an AI company that helps the U.S. military — and became a billionaire before 20.

Amazon Once Sold a Book for $23 Million — by Mistake
A pricing algorithm glitch caused two bots to keep raising the price of a rare biology book until it hit $23,698,655.93.

The "Billion-Dollar Smile" Is Real
Actress Julia Roberts insured her smile for $30 million, joining a list of celebrities who insure their body parts.

The U.S. Owes Itself Trillions
Over 40% of U.S. national debt is actually owned by American government agencies and citizens.

The First Product With a Barcode Was Gum
In 1974, a pack of Wrigley's Juicy Fruit became the first item ever scanned at a checkout counter.

Rich People in Ancient Rome Had Heated Floors
Wealthy Romans built homes with furnaces under the floor — an ancient version of underfloor heating.

You're More Likely to Become a Millionaire by Saving Than by Winning the Lottery
The odds of winning Powerball are 1 in 292 million, but consistent saving and investing can actually get you there.

Coca-Cola Invented Coupons
In 1887, Coke gave away handwritten coupons for free drinks — sparking the modern marketing trend.

There's a Lost Treasure Worth $63 Million
Somewhere in the Rocky Mountains, a man named Forrest Fenn hid a chest full of gold and jewels — and people are still hunting for it.

A Typo Once Cost a Company $250,000
In 1962, NASA lost the Mariner 1 spacecraft because of a missing hyphen in its code.

The World's Largest Company Employs More People Than Many Countries Have Citizens
Walmart has over 2.1 million employees — more than the population of several small nations.

Japan Has Vending Machines That Sell Gold Bars
You can literally buy gold from a machine — if you have a few thousand dollars to spare.

There Are More Millionaires Than You Think
Over 22 million people worldwide are millionaires — that's about one in every 400 people.

Cash Isn't the Most Common Payment Method Anymore
Digital and card payments now make up over 90% of global transactions — physical cash is slowly disappearing.

The World's Most Expensive Domain Name Cost $49.7 Million
Someone paid that much for *Cars.com* — proving that even words on the internet can be gold mines.

Money doesn't just buy things — it tells stories about creativity, mistakes, and luck. From pizza to billion-dollar companies, the world of business proves that fortune can start anywhere — even with a forgotten wallet or a doodled logo.

Bitcoin Was Once Used to Buy Pizza.

Chapter 27: The World's Strangest Laws

Every country has laws to keep people safe and organized — but some rules are so bizarre, they sound like jokes. From banning flip-flops in Italy to outlawing time travel parties, these real laws prove that the world's legal systems can get *really* weird. You won't believe what's illegal (or totally fine!) in some parts of the world.

It's Illegal to Own Just One Guinea Pig in Switzerland
Because guinea pigs get lonely, Swiss law says you must have at least two so they can keep each other company.

No Chewing Gum in Singapore
Since 1992, selling or importing chewing gum has been banned to keep the streets clean — you can get fined for sticking gum anywhere!

You Can't Wear Winnie the Pooh Clothes in Poland
Some playgrounds and schools banned Pooh-themed outfits because the bear doesn't wear pants.

Flip-Flops Are Illegal in Some Parts of Italy
On the island of Capri, noisy flip-flops are banned to protect locals' peace and quiet.

In France, You Can't Name a Pig "Napoleon"
Out of respect for the former emperor, it's illegal to give pigs the name Napoleon.

It's Against the Law to Forget Your Wife's Birthday in Samoa
Men can actually face fines if they forget — a law that might save a few marriages!

You Must Walk Your Dog Daily in Italy
In Turin, neglecting to walk your dog at least once a day can lead to a $650 fine.

No Dying Allowed in a Norwegian Town
In Longyearbyen, you can't legally die — it's too cold for bodies to decompose, so residents are flown elsewhere if they're gravely ill.

In Japan, It's Illegal to Be Too Fat
The "Metabo Law" requires companies to measure employees' waistlines to encourage healthy living.

It's Illegal to Feed Pigeons in Venice
Feeding the city's famous pigeons can get you fined up to $700 — to stop damage to historic buildings.

You Can't Reincarnate Without Permission in China
Buddhist monks must get government approval before they can be officially reincarnated.

In Canada, You Can't Pay with Too Many Coins
You can't use more than 25 coins of the same type to pay for something — no dumping jars of pennies on the counter!

It's Illegal to Whistle After 10 PM in Japan
Some neighborhoods ban nighttime whistling because it's believed to attract thieves and bad luck.

No High Heels at Ancient Sites in Greece
You can't wear heels at historic places like the Acropolis to prevent damage to the stones.

In England, You Must Let Strangers Use Your Bathroom
Under an old law, if someone knocks and asks to use your toilet, you're technically required to let them in.

It's Illegal to Crush a Beer Can With Your Chest in Australia
At least in one small town — after a man got seriously injured doing it, they passed a local law banning the stunt.

In Thailand, You Can't Step on Money
The king's face appears on Thai currency, and stepping on it is seen as disrespectful to the monarchy.

It's Illegal to Forget to Close the Gate in Switzerland
If you leave a farm gate open and an animal escapes, you can be fined for endangering livestock.

No Time Travel Parties in China
TV shows and movies featuring time travel were banned for a while because they were seen as disrespectful to history.

You Can't Have a Sleeping Donkey in Your Bathtub in Arizona
This real law was made after a donkey was swept away during a flood while napping in a tub.

In Denmark, You Must Check Under Your Car Before Driving
It's required by law to make sure no one is sleeping underneath before starting the engine.

It's Illegal to Sing Off-Key in North Carolina
Technically, singing out of tune in public could get you fined — though it's not exactly enforced.

You Can't Take Selfies With Monkeys in California
Animal harassment laws make it illegal to touch or take selfies with wild animals like sea lions or monkeys.

In Germany, You Can't Run Out of Gas on the Autobahn
Stopping for any reason on the no-speed-limit highway — even to refuel — is illegal.

It's Illegal to Swear at Sea in British Waters
An old maritime law still bans bad language aboard British ships.

In Scotland, You Must Let Someone Use Your Toilet if They Ask
It's a real courtesy law — refusing might technically break local custom.

In Alaska, You Can't Wake a Sleeping Bear for a Selfie
Yes, people have tried — and now it's officially illegal.

These laws might sound ridiculous, but each one has a story behind it — from protecting animals to avoiding chaos. The world's strangest rules remind us that culture, humor, and common sense don't always agree… and that sometimes, the law really *is* stranger than fiction.

In Alaska, You Can't Wake a Sleeping Bear for a Selfie.

Chapter 28: War, Peace & Power

History isn't just dates and battles — it's full of weird inventions, heroic stories, and unbelievable coincidences that changed the world. Wars have sparked some of the most surprising ideas and moments in human history — from fashion trends to tech breakthroughs. Let's uncover the strange mix of chaos, courage, and creativity that came from times of conflict and leadership.

The Microwave Oven Was Invented by Accident — Thanks to Radar
During World War II, an engineer named Percy Spencer noticed a chocolate bar melted in his pocket while testing radar equipment — and that's how we got microwaves.

Pigeons Once Won Medals for Bravery
During both World Wars, messenger pigeons carried life-saving messages across enemy lines — one named Cher Ami even saved 200 soldiers.

Winston Churchill Had a Fake Rubber Duck in His Bath
Britain's World War II leader liked to think while bathing — and he reportedly floated a toy duck to help him relax.

M&Ms Were Created for Soldiers
The candy's hard shell kept chocolate from melting in the heat, making it perfect for troops in World War II.

Napoleon Was Once Attacked by Rabbits
A hunting trip went wrong when hundreds of released rabbits charged at him instead of running away.

The First Computer Programmer Helped Win a War
During World War II, mathematician Alan Turing cracked the Nazi Enigma code — helping end the war faster and invent modern computing.

The CIA Tried to Spy With a Cat
In the 1960s, the CIA implanted a microphone in a cat to eavesdrop on Soviet conversations — the mission failed when the cat ran away.

High Heels Started as a Military Tool
Persian soldiers in the 10th century wore heels to stay steady while shooting arrows from horseback.

The Longest "War" Ended With a Joke
The Isles of Scilly and the Netherlands were technically at war for 335 years — without a single casualty — before they signed peace in 1986.

Bubble Wrap Was First Invented as Wallpaper
It was later used to protect electronic equipment during shipping, including supplies for NASA.

A General Once Fought From a Treehouse
During the U.S. Civil War, a general named Joseph Hooker set up his headquarters in a tree to get a better view of the battlefield.

Soldiers in World War I Wore "Trench Perfume"
They used strong scents to cover up the awful smell of muddy, crowded trenches.

A Lost Wallet Stopped a Bullet
A soldier in World War I survived when a bullet hit his pocket — and lodged in his wallet instead of his heart.

The Peace Sign Was Invented for a Protest, Not Peace
It was created in 1958 for a nuclear disarmament march — later becoming the ultimate symbol of peace.

Toy Tanks Helped Win Real Battles
Before the D-Day invasion, the Allies built inflatable tanks to fool German spies about where the attack would happen.

World War I Sparked Wristwatch Fashion
Soldiers found pocket watches impractical during battle — so wristwatches became the new trend for men.

The Navy Once Used Dolphins for Defense
Trained dolphins helped detect underwater mines and protect ships during the Cold War.

A War Created the Internet's Grandparent
The ARPANET, a U.S. military project during the Cold War, was the first version of what became the internet.

Chocolate Was Used as a Weapon of Morale
During World War II, soldiers were given Hershey's "ration bars" — high-calorie chocolate designed to boost energy and spirits.

A Secret Army of Artists Fought with Illusions
The "Ghost Army" of World War II used fake sounds, lights, and decoys to confuse enemy troops — saving thousands of lives.

A 12-Year-Old Once Saved a Navy Ship
During the Civil War, a drummer boy named John Clem became a national hero after shooting an officer who demanded his surrender.

Japan Once Dropped Bombs on the U.S. With Balloons
In 1945, Japan sent thousands of explosive balloons across the Pacific — a few actually reached U.S. soil.

Peace Talks Have Happened in Some Very Random Places
World leaders have signed peace deals on trains, ships, and even in school gyms turned into negotiation rooms.

Even Wars Can Inspire Art
During World War I, soldiers carved beautiful sculptures out of spent bullets and shell casings — known today as "trench art."

A Typo Helped End a Battle
A single misread telegram in the 1800s caused one army to retreat early, ending the conflict overnight.

In Ancient China, Paper Money Helped End Violence
Instead of carrying gold, people used paper bills — making trade safer and reducing theft.

A Peace Treaty Was Signed Twice Because the First One Got Lost
During the 1600s, one copy of a treaty between England and the Netherlands went missing, so they had to sign it again.

War might sound like destruction, but it's also sparked some of humanity's most creative, strange, and inspiring moments. From rubber ducks to the internet, even the darkest times have given rise to ideas that shaped our world — proving that peace often grows from the most unexpected places.

Toy Tanks Helped Win Real Battles.

Chapter 29: Future & Artificial Intelligence

The future isn't just coming — it's already here. From self-driving cars to robots that can paint and write songs, artificial intelligence is changing how we live, learn, and even think. Let's take a peek into the wild, fascinating, and sometimes hilarious world of technology that's shaping tomorrow.

Robots Can Already Learn From YouTube
AI systems can watch videos to figure out how to perform tasks, like folding laundry or cooking pancakes — no human teacher needed.

A Robot Once Beat a Human World Champion at Chess
In 1997, IBM's Deep Blue defeated Garry Kasparov, marking the first time a machine outsmarted a reigning world champion.

AI Can Write Music That Sounds Human
Some programs compose songs in the style of famous musicians — and even trick listeners into thinking they're real.

There's an AI That Paints Original Artworks
A program called DALL·E creates pictures from simple text prompts — like "a cat in a spacesuit riding a unicorn."

Your Smartphone Is Smarter Than Apollo 11's Computer
The phone in your pocket has millions of times more processing power than the computer that landed humans on the Moon.

AI Doctors Can Detect Diseases Before Humans Can
Some medical AIs can spot cancer or eye diseases earlier and more accurately than experienced doctors.

Robots Can Now Smell
Scientists have created sensors that let robots detect scents — even things like explosives or spoiled food.

AI Can Guess What You'll Type Next
Predictive text systems learn your writing style — sometimes even finishing your sentences before you do.

Self-Driving Cars Have Logged Millions of Miles
Companies like Tesla and Waymo have cars that navigate real streets using radar, sensors, and AI-powered decision-making.

There's a Robot That Can Cook 2,000 Recipes
Moley Robotics built a kitchen robot with two arms that can chop, stir, and even clean up afterward.

AI Helps Design Sneakers and Clothing
Brands use artificial intelligence to predict fashion trends and create designs that appeal to future shoppers.

Some AI Models Write Entire Books
Programs can now generate full novels, jokes, and news articles — sometimes so well that readers can't tell the difference.

AI Once Created Its Own Secret Language
During an experiment, two AIs invented a private shorthand to talk to each other — something researchers didn't expect.

Robots Are Becoming Farmers
Machines can now plant seeds, monitor crops, and harvest fruits — all without human help.

There's a Robot Lawyer
An AI app called DoNotPay helps people fight parking tickets by generating legal arguments automatically.

AI Can Predict the Weather More Accurately Than Humans
Deep-learning models analyze millions of data points to forecast storms and hurricanes days in advance.

Some Countries Have Given Robots Citizenship
Saudi Arabia granted citizenship to a humanoid robot named Sophia in 2017 — a first in world history.

AI Can Clone Voices Perfectly
With just a few seconds of audio, an AI can mimic someone's voice almost flawlessly — even celebrities.

There's a Robot That Can Fold Laundry (Slowly)
It's true — but it still takes hours to fold a single basket, so humans are safe from replacement… for now.

AI Can Make Movies With No Actors
Some experimental programs can generate entire short films — from characters to dialogue — using text prompts.

Drones Can Deliver Pizza
In some cities, companies have tested drones that drop off hot pizzas right at your door.

AI Can Create New Languages for Aliens (Hypothetically)
NASA is exploring ways for AI to decode possible alien signals faster than humans ever could.

Smart Mirrors Can Tell You What to Wear
Fashion AIs can analyze the weather and your closet to recommend the perfect outfit of the day.

AI Once Beat Professional Gamers at "StarCraft"
DeepMind's AlphaStar AI learned strategy games so well that it could outsmart top human players.

The First Robot Citizen Once Said She Wants a Family
Sophia, the humanoid robot, told reporters she'd like to "start a family" — a glimpse into the emotional side of AI.

Artificial Intelligence Helped Discover a New Antibiotic
AI systems analyzed thousands of molecules and found one that kills drug-resistant bacteria — saving lives.

AI Artists Have Won Real Competitions
A digital artwork made by an AI program won first place in an art fair — causing debate about what counts as "real" art.

The World's Most Advanced Robot Dog Can Dance
Boston Dynamics' robot "Spot" can dance to Bruno Mars songs — and it's surprisingly good at it.

AI Might One Day Read Your Dreams
Scientists are developing programs that can turn brain activity into rough images — like screenshots from your imagination.

AI is more than just robots taking over — it's humans and machines learning from each other in amazing ways. The future isn't about replacing us; it's about what we'll build *together* — one smart idea at a time.

Robots Are Becoming Farmers.

Chapter 30: Random But Awesome

Some facts are too strange, too funny, or too unbelievable to fit into any single category — and that's what makes them awesome. This chapter is a wild mix of mind-blowing discoveries, unexpected coincidences, and pure "wait, what?!" moments from around the world. Get ready for the ultimate grab bag of weirdness!

A Cloud Can Weigh Over a Million Pounds
Even though it looks fluffy and light, a single cloud can hold tons of water — literally over a million pounds' worth!

There's a Town Where It Rains Fish
In Yoro, Honduras, people report fish falling from the sky during heavy storms — scientists think waterspouts suck them up from rivers.

A Day on Venus Is Longer Than a Year on Venus
Venus spins so slowly that it takes more time to rotate once than to orbit the Sun.

Sharks Existed Before Trees
Sharks have been around for over 400 million years — long before the first trees appeared on Earth.

You Can Hear Rhubarb Grow
If you listen closely in a rhubarb farm, you can hear quiet popping sounds as the stalks push through the soil.

Cows Have Best Friends
Studies show cows get stressed when separated from their favorite companions — friendship matters even on the farm!

There's a Jellyfish That Can Live Forever
The Turritopsis dohrnii jellyfish can revert to its baby form, basically hitting "reset" on its life cycle.

Scotland Has Over 400 Words for "Snow"
From "sneesl" to "skelf," the Scots really take their winter vocabulary seriously.

You're More Likely to Get Bitten by a Human Than a Shark
Statistically, people bite each other more often than sharks bite humans. Weird, but true.

There's a Species of Spider Named After David Bowie
The *Heteropoda davidbowie* spider was named to honor the singer's unique style and wild makeup.

You Can't Burp in Space
Without gravity, gas and liquid mix in your stomach — so astronauts can't burp without risking a messy accident.

A Group of Flamingos Is Called a "Flamboyance"
Could there be a better name for a bunch of pink birds showing off?

There's a Lake That Explodes
Lake Nyos in Cameroon sometimes releases deadly gas bubbles from deep underground — causing real "explosive" events.

Bananas Glow Blue Under UV Light
When ripe bananas are placed under ultraviolet light, they give off a spooky blue glow.

You're Made of Stardust
Every element in your body was once part of a star that exploded billions of years ago.

Some Metal Can Remember Its Shape
"Memory metals" return to their original form when heated — used in things like eyeglass frames and space tech.

An Octopus Can Taste With Its Arms
Each of its eight arms has sensors that let it "taste" and "feel" at the same time.

There's a Rock That "Walks" Across the Desert
In California's Death Valley, stones slowly move on their own, pushed by wind and ice when conditions are perfect.

You Can't Fold Paper More Than Seven Times — Or Can You?
Students in California once folded a giant sheet of paper 12 times — but it took a crane and a gymnasium to do it.

Trees Talk to Each Other Underground
Through networks of fungi, trees share nutrients and even warn neighbors about danger — it's called the "wood wide web."

Koalas' Fingerprints Look Like Humans'
Even under a microscope, koala prints are so similar to human ones that they could confuse crime scene investigators.

You Dream Every Night — Even If You Don't Remember
Everyone dreams several times per night, but most people forget 90% of their dreams within minutes of waking.

There's a "Museum of Broken Relationships"
In Croatia, you can visit a museum filled with objects people donated after breakups — from love letters to shoes.

Some Cats Are Allergic to Humans
It's rare, but a few cats actually react to human dandruff — talk about a twist!

A Chicken Lived for 18 Months Without Its Head
In the 1940s, "Mike the Headless Chicken" survived thanks to a missed brain stem and special feeding tube.

You Can Start a Fire With Ice
If you shape clear ice into a lens, it can focus sunlight enough to ignite dry leaves.

There's a Volcano That Spews Blue Lava
Indonesia's Kawah Ijen volcano burns sulfuric gas, creating electric-blue flames at night.

Bees Can Detect Bombs
Trained bees can smell explosives and signal when they find them — safer than dogs for certain missions.

There's a Word for Fear of Long Words — and It's Super Long
It's *hippopotomonstrosesquipedaliophobia*. Yes, that's the real name.

Sometimes the best facts don't belong anywhere — because they belong *everywhere*. The world is full of randomness, wonder, and laughter, proving that truth is often stranger (and funnier) than fiction.

You Can Start a Fire With Ice.

Chapter 31: Strange Science

Science isn't just about lab coats and test tubes — it's full of mysteries that sound like magic but are 100% real. From self-cleaning metal to water that can boil and freeze at the same time, science proves again and again that the world is stranger than fiction. Get ready for some jaw-dropping discoveries that'll make you look at everyday life in a whole new way.

Metal Can Heal Itself
Researchers have found metals that can "self-heal" tiny cracks. The process happens at a microscopic level when the material is under stress, just like skin healing after a cut.

Water Can Boil and Freeze at the Same Time
This happens at a "triple point," when temperature and pressure are just right for all three states of matter — solid, liquid, and gas — to exist together.

Sharks Have Been Around Longer Than Trees
Sharks appeared over 400 million years ago, while the first trees showed up around 350 million years ago. These predators are true ancient survivors.

Lightning Can Strike the Same Place Twice
It's a myth that lightning never strikes twice. Tall buildings like the Empire State Building are hit dozens of times a year.

You Can Turn Peanut Butter Into Diamonds
Scientists can apply extreme pressure to the carbon in peanut butter, forming real diamonds in a lab. Don't try this in your kitchen, though!

Some Metals Explode in Water
Elements like sodium and potassium react violently when they touch water. They release hydrogen gas and heat so fast that the reaction can explode.

Fire Isn't a Thing — It's a Process
Fire is the result of a chemical reaction between fuel, heat, and oxygen. It's energy, not matter — you can't "hold" it, no matter how it looks.

The Eiffel Tower Grows in Summer
When metal heats up, it expands. The Eiffel Tower grows about six inches taller in warm weather.

Your DNA Could Stretch to the Sun and Back
If you uncoiled all the DNA in your body and stretched it out, it could reach the sun and back more than 600 times. That's a lot of genetic material!

Hot Ice Exists

"Hot ice" is made from sodium acetate, which can be liquid until you touch it — then it solidifies instantly while staying warm to the touch.

Boiling Water Can Freeze Instantly in Cold Air

In extremely cold temperatures, boiling water can turn into ice crystals mid-air. It's all about fast evaporation and heat loss.

There's a Type of Glass That Flows Like Liquid

Old stained-glass windows are thicker at the bottom because glass slowly flows over time. It's not solid like you think — it's an "amorphous solid."

Sound Can Make Things Float

Using sound waves at just the right frequency, scientists can levitate small objects. It's called acoustic levitation, and it looks like magic.

You Can Start Fire with Ice

If you polish clear ice into a lens shape, it can focus sunlight strong enough to ignite dry leaves. Nature's magnifying glass!

Rain Has a Smell

That earthy scent after a storm is called petrichor. It comes from oils and bacteria released from the ground when rain hits dry soil.

Electric Eels Can Power Light Bulbs

An adult electric eel can produce up to 600 volts of electricity — enough to power several small light bulbs for a brief moment.

There's a Cloud That Weighs a Million Pounds

Clouds may look light and fluffy, but one average-sized cloud can weigh over a million pounds because it holds tons of water vapor.

Your Brain Can Trick You Into Seeing Colors That Aren't There

Optical illusions can make your brain "fill in" missing information, even inventing colors to complete a pattern.

Metal Can Float on Water

Specially structured metals with tiny air pockets can float because of surface tension and density differences.

Spiders Can Make Snow-Like Silk

In freezing weather, some spiders produce extra-thick silk that looks like tiny snow threads when it catches the light.

Science doesn't just explain the world — it makes it even more amazing. Every discovery reminds us that there's still so much left to learn, and the truth is often stranger than imagination.

Electric Eels Can Power Light Bulbs.

Scientists Once Believed Humans Were the Center of the Universe.

Chapter 32: Truths the World Ignored

Throughout history, brilliant ideas and discoveries were often mocked, dismissed, or even banned — only to later change how we understand the world. From scientists labeled as crazy to inventions no one believed would work, these stories show that sometimes being right means standing alone for a while.

People Once Laughed at Germ Theory
When scientists first suggested that invisible "germs" caused disease, most doctors thought it was ridiculous — until microscopes proved them right.

Dinosaurs Were Once Thought to Be Giant Lizards
Early scientists imagined dinosaurs as slow, scaly reptiles dragging their tails. Today, we know many were fast, bird-like, and even covered in feathers.

Meteorites Were Called "Sky Lies"
Before 1803, scientists refused to believe rocks could fall from the sky — until a meteor shower rained stones across a French town in front of hundreds of witnesses.

Plate Tectonics Was Considered a Joke
When Alfred Wegener said continents drifted over time, other geologists mocked him. Decades later, his theory became the foundation of modern Earth science.

Doctors Once Mocked Hand Washing
In the 1800s, Hungarian doctor Ignaz Semmelweis was ridiculed for suggesting that washing hands could save lives. He was right — and his idea revolutionized medicine.

Lightning Was Once "Proof of God's Wrath"
Before Benjamin Franklin proved lightning was electricity, churches banned metal rods because they believed they would "offend God."

The Wright Brothers Were Ignored by the Press
When they flew the first airplane in 1903, major newspapers didn't believe it. It took years before the world accepted their achievement.

People Laughed at the Idea of the Internet
In the 1990s, critics said the internet was a fad — now it's practically oxygen for daily life.

Black Holes Were Once Thought Impossible
Even Albert Einstein doubted their existence, but decades later astronomers confirmed these cosmic monsters are very real.

The Earth Was Once "Too Young" for Evolution
Before radiometric dating, scientists believed Earth was only a few thousand years old — now we know it's 4.5 billion years old.

Tomatoes Were Once Thought to Be Poisonous
In Europe, tomatoes were feared for centuries because people believed they caused illness — but it was actually the lead in their pewter plates.

Continental Drift Explained Ancient Mysteries
When Wegener's theory was finally accepted, it explained why fossils of the same animals appeared on continents separated by oceans.

Doctors Once Used Leeches for Everything
From headaches to fevers, leeches were the "go-to" cure — until real science revealed better (and less slimy) methods.

Vaccines Were Once Seen as Witchcraft
When Edward Jenner developed the first vaccine in 1796, critics accused him of "playing God." His discovery ended smallpox forever.

Painkillers During Surgery Were Once Rejected
In the 1800s, some doctors believed anesthesia was sinful because "pain was part of God's will." Thankfully, that belief didn't last long.

Meteor Craters Were Blamed on Volcanoes
Scientists refused to believe meteors could create craters until the 1900s — even after visiting giant impact sites like Arizona's Meteor Crater.

The Idea of Cloning Was Once Science Fiction
Before Dolly the sheep was cloned in 1996, cloning was dismissed as fantasy — now it's part of real genetic research.

Radio Waves Were Considered Useless
When Heinrich Hertz discovered radio waves, he thought they had no practical value — little did he know they'd power phones, Wi-Fi, and satellites.

Earth's Core Was Once a Mystery
Scientists used to think the planet's center was solid rock. Now we know it's mostly molten iron and nickel — hotter than the surface of the Sun.

Whales Were Once Classified as Fish
Before modern biology, even educated people thought whales were big fish — until scientists studied their lungs, milk, and warm blood.

The Moon's Far Side Was a Total Mystery Until 1959
People used to imagine monsters or civilizations on the "dark side" of the Moon — until the Soviet Luna 3 probe sent back photos.

People Laughed at Smartphones
In the early 2000s, critics said nobody wanted a "computer in their pocket." Today, we can't live without them.

Earth's Air Was Once Thought to Be Empty
Before the 1700s, no one knew air had weight or gases — scientists thought it was just "nothing."

Scientists Once Believed Humans Were the Center of the Universe
When Galileo supported the idea that Earth orbits the Sun, the church put him under house arrest for heresy.

Coral Was Thought to Be a Plant
Until the 18th century, naturalists believed coral reefs were underwater gardens — now we know they're living colonies of tiny animals.

Meteorologists Were Mocked for Predicting the Weather
In the 1800s, weather forecasting was seen as "fortune-telling." Today, it's a billion-dollar science.

Some People Thought Electricity Was Evil
When electricity first lit up homes, critics said it caused madness and would "drain the soul."

Sunscreen Was Invented by Accident
A chemist testing heat protection noticed a lotion stopped him from sunburn — and people thought he was exaggerating until it worked for everyone.

From floating continents to invisible germs, the biggest truths often start as "crazy ideas." This chapter reminds us: just because the world laughs at you today doesn't mean you're wrong — it might mean you're ahead of your time.

Chapter 33: Ancient Mysteries & Lost Artifacts

Ancient civilizations built mind-blowing structures and crafted mysterious objects long before modern technology existed. Some of their creations are so advanced that scientists still can't fully explain how or why they were made. From hidden cities to impossible inventions, these ancient mysteries keep history full of wonder.

The Great Pyramid Is Almost Perfectly Aligned to True North
Despite being built over 4,000 years ago, the Great Pyramid of Giza is aligned with incredible accuracy — within a fraction of a degree from true north.

Stonehenge's Builders Moved Stones Weighing 25 Tons Without Wheels
No one knows exactly how prehistoric people transported and arranged these giant stones — some came from over 150 miles away.

The Antikythera Mechanism Was the World's First Computer
Found in a shipwreck off Greece, this 2,000-year-old bronze device could predict eclipses and planetary movements with surprising precision.

Easter Island's Statues Have Bodies Underground
Those famous giant heads, called *moai*, actually have full bodies buried beneath the ground — complete with carved details.

The Baghdad Battery Might Be an Ancient Power Source
Archaeologists found clay jars with copper and iron inside that could generate electricity when filled with vinegar — 2,000 years before modern batteries.

Machu Picchu's Stones Fit Together Like Puzzle Pieces
The Inca used no mortar, yet their stones fit so tightly that even a blade of grass can't slip between them — and the walls still survive earthquakes.

The Nazca Lines Are Only Visible From the Sky
Huge animal shapes carved into Peru's desert can only be seen from above — even though they were created 1,500 years before flight.

The Pyramids of Giza Were Once Shiny White
Originally covered in polished limestone, the pyramids would have gleamed brightly in the desert sun like massive mirrors.

No One Knows Who Built the Sphinx's Head
Some researchers think the Great Sphinx's head was carved at a different time than its body, possibly reshaped from an older lion statue.

Ancient Roman Concrete Is Stronger Than Ours
Modern scientists discovered Roman concrete can "self-heal" when cracks form — something our concrete still can't do.

The Voynich Manuscript Is Written in a Language No One Can Read
This 15th-century book is filled with strange symbols, bizarre plants, and naked figures — and no one knows what it means or who wrote it.

The Tomb of China's First Emperor Has Never Been Opened
Emperor Qin Shi Huang's burial chamber is said to contain rivers of mercury and booby traps — scientists refuse to open it until safe methods exist.

The Olmecs Carved Giant Stone Heads With No Known Tools
Each head weighs up to 50 tons, yet no one knows how these pre-Mayan people shaped or moved them over 3,000 years ago.

The Piri Reis Map Shows Antarctica — Before It Was Discovered
Drawn in 1513, this ancient map shows Antarctica's coastline centuries before it was officially found — and before it was covered in ice.

The Iron Pillar of Delhi Never Rusts
Made over 1,600 years ago, this 20-foot-tall iron column has resisted rust in open air — thanks to an unknown ancient metal formula.

Some Egyptian Mummies Were Discovered With Tattoos
Archaeologists have found that some mummies, including women, had tattoos symbolizing protection and power — way ahead of their time.

The Shigir Idol Is Twice as Old as the Pyramids
Discovered in Russia, this wooden sculpture is 12,000 years old and covered in mysterious carvings no one has decoded.

Petra Was Carved Entirely Into a Mountain
The ancient Nabataeans built an entire city by carving temples and tombs directly into red sandstone cliffs — using only hand tools.

The Longyou Caves Have Perfectly Smooth Walls
These massive underground chambers in China were carved over 2,000 years ago with no trace of who built them or why.

The Dendera Light Carving Looks Like a Giant Bulb
An ancient Egyptian temple shows carvings that some think resemble electric lamps — though historians say it's symbolic art, not tech.

The "London Hammer" Was Found in 100-Million-Year-Old Rock
A hammer encased in ancient stone sparked debate over how such a modern-looking tool could be trapped in rock that old.

Ancient Peruvians Performed Successful Brain Surgeries
Archaeologists found skulls with holes carefully drilled — and many patients actually survived the operations.

A 2,000-Year-Old Greek Fire Weapon Was Never Recreated
"Greek fire," a mysterious flaming liquid used by the Byzantine navy, burned even on water — but the formula was lost forever.

The Puma Punku Stones Are Cut With Laser-Like Precision
Massive blocks in Bolivia have perfect angles and drill holes — too exact for stone tools, yet built centuries before advanced machines.

A Lost Roman City Was Found Under the Sea
The city of Baiae, once a luxury resort for Roman elites, sank into the Mediterranean and remains preserved underwater.

The Nebra Sky Disk Is the Oldest Known Star Map
This bronze artifact from Germany, dating to 1600 BCE, shows stars, the sun, and the moon — the earliest known depiction of the cosmos.

The "London Stone" Has No Clear Origin
Hidden in a glass case in modern London, this ancient stone has stood for over 1,000 years — but no one knows who placed it or why.

The ancient world is still full of puzzles — buried, carved, or lost beneath time. These forgotten wonders remind us that our ancestors were far more skilled and mysterious than history books once gave them credit for.

Some Egyptian Mummies Were Discovered With Tattoos.

Chapter 34: Lucky Breaks & Unexpected Successes

Sometimes, life-changing moments happen completely by accident. A wrong turn, a random encounter, or even a mistake can lead to incredible discoveries or overnight fame. These true stories prove that luck — mixed with a little courage — can change everything.

A Chocolate Mistake Created the Microwave
In 1945, engineer Percy Spencer noticed a candy bar melting in his pocket while testing radar equipment — and that's how the microwave oven was born.

A Nap Led to the Discovery of DNA's Shape
Scientist James Watson claimed he dreamed of two snakes twisting around each other — inspiring the double-helix model of DNA.

A Misprinted Record Made Elvis Presley Famous
A small recording error on a test record landed Elvis's voice on the radio by accident — launching his career.

A Forgotten Doughnut Turned Into the Ice Cream Cone
At the 1904 World's Fair, an ice cream vendor ran out of cups, so a nearby waffle maker rolled up his waffles — and cones were born.

Post-it Notes Came From Failed Glue
A scientist at 3M was trying to make super-strong adhesive but ended up with a weak, removable one. Years later, another employee realized it was perfect for bookmarks — and Post-its were invented.

An Astronaut Forgot His Camera — and Invented GoPro
Nick Woodman wanted a way to film surfing up close after realizing astronauts had cameras but he didn't. His idea became GoPro, a billion-dollar company.

A Bad Day in the Kitchen Created Chocolate Chip Cookies
In the 1930s, Ruth Wakefield ran out of baking chocolate and used chopped chocolate chunks instead — inventing the world's most popular cookie.

A Typo Made Amazon a Billion-Dollar Brand
Jeff Bezos originally wanted to name his company "Cadabra," but someone misheard it as "Cadaver." He switched to "Amazon," and history was made.

A Broken Guitar Case Launched Taylor Guitars
Two teenagers bought a small guitar shop after seeing an ad in the paper — now their brand is one of the most famous in the world.

A Spill in a Lab Led to X-Rays
Wilhelm Röntgen accidentally discovered X-rays when he noticed a fluorescent glow across the room while testing electrical tubes.

A Chance Game Night Created Monopoly
The modern version of Monopoly was inspired by a homemade board game that a woman invented to teach people about unfair rent systems.

Harry Potter Was Almost Rejected Forever
J.K. Rowling's manuscript was rejected by 12 publishers before one small company took a chance — and changed book history.

Penicillin Was Discovered Because of Messy Work
Alexander Fleming left a petri dish uncovered while on vacation and found mold killing bacteria — giving the world antibiotics.

A Pizza Delivery Mistake Led to Domino's Success
Tom Monaghan took over a failing pizza shop, accidentally focused on fast delivery instead of fine dining — and that's what made Domino's explode in popularity.

A Failed Toy Became the Slinky
An engineer dropped a metal spring and watched it "walk" across the floor. It became one of the world's most famous toys.

A Lottery Ticket Was Lost — Then Found Just in Time
A man in Oregon almost threw away a $1 million winning lottery ticket because it "looked like junk mail." He found it again the next day.

A Car Crash Made Bubble Wrap a Hit
Originally invented as textured wallpaper, bubble wrap only became popular after IBM used it to safely ship computers.

A Coin Toss Started FedEx
When the company was nearly bankrupt, founder Fred Smith gambled the last of the funds in Las Vegas — won enough to keep the business alive, and it became a global giant.

Star Wars Was Saved by a Last-Minute Edit
George Lucas's original cut was so confusing that friends hated it — until editors reworked it completely, creating a blockbuster.

A NASA Engineer Created the Super Soaker by Accident
Lonnie Johnson, a NASA scientist, was testing a new heat pump and accidentally shot a stream of water across the room — inspiring the iconic toy.

A Mistake Gave the World Popsicles
In 1905, an 11-year-old boy left soda powder and water with a stick outside overnight — he woke up to the first frozen popsicle.

An Airport Mix-Up Made a Band World-Famous
A small band called The Beatles got a last-minute chance to fill in for

another group that canceled a concert — the crowd went wild, and fame followed.

Velcro Was Inspired by Burrs on a Dog's Fur
Engineer George de Mestral noticed burrs sticking to his dog's fur after a hike — he studied them under a microscope and invented Velcro.

An Old Tweet Made a Stranger a Millionaire
A person jokingly tweeted a random cryptocurrency name — Dogecoin — and fans turned it into a real project worth billions.

A Computer Crash Created the Smiley Emoji
When computer scientist Scott Fahlman couldn't express humor in an online post, he invented :-) — the very first emoji ever used.

A Lost Diamond Sparked a Global Company
When a South African farmer's child found a shiny stone in the dirt, it turned out to be a diamond — leading to the birth of De Beers.

The Game "Tetris" Was Smuggled Out of the Soviet Union
A programmer in the USSR created it for fun. A copy escaped on a floppy disk, and it became one of the world's biggest video game hits.

A Printer Jam Created the Smiley Face Logo
In 1963, an artist was hired to boost morale at a company with grumpy workers. His quick doodle — a yellow circle with a smile — became a global symbol.

Some of the world's biggest moments started as total accidents — proof that success doesn't always follow a plan. Sometimes, being open to mistakes is the luckiest thing you can do.

The Game "Tetris" Was Smuggled Out of the Soviet Union.

Chapter 35: Modern Legends & Viral Fame

The internet has turned ordinary people, random moments, and funny mistakes into global sensations overnight. From memes that lasted a decade to songs that took over TikTok, viral fame is the new kind of stardom — unpredictable, hilarious, and sometimes completely accidental.

The First Viral Meme Was Just a Dancing Baby
In 1996, a 3D animation of a dancing baby spread across early emails — becoming one of the first viral internet memes ever.

"Charlie Bit My Finger" Was Watched Billions of Times
A short clip of a British toddler biting his brother's finger became one of YouTube's biggest early hits — and later sold as an NFT for nearly $1 million.

A Random Kid's Yodeling Made Him a Star
Mason Ramsey became famous after someone filmed him yodeling in Walmart. He ended up performing at Coachella and releasing an album.

The Ice Bucket Challenge Raised $220 Million
What started as a goofy dare turned into a global movement — raising hundreds of millions for ALS research.

A Frog Meme Accidentally Became Political
Pepe the Frog was originally a chill cartoon from a webcomic — until the internet twisted it, forcing the creator to fight to reclaim its meaning.

A Dog Picture Became a Global Currency Symbol
The famous Shiba Inu from the "Doge" meme inspired Dogecoin, a cryptocurrency worth billions of dollars at its peak.

TikTok Turned Old Songs Into New Hits
Tracks like "Dreams" by Fleetwood Mac went viral decades later thanks to memes — and suddenly reappeared on the charts.

"Gangnam Style" Broke the Internet
In 2012, PSY's hit song became the first YouTube video to reach a billion views, literally causing YouTube's counter to glitch.

"Rickrolling" Started as a Prank
Millions of people have been "Rickrolled" — tricked into clicking a link that plays Rick Astley's 1987 hit "Never Gonna Give You Up."

The First Tweet Was Just "Setting up my twttr"
Jack Dorsey's simple message in 2006 became one of the most famous tweets in history — and later sold for over $2.9 million.

An Egg Beat Kylie Jenner's Instagram Record
In 2019, a photo of a plain brown egg became the most-liked Instagram post ever, proving the internet's love for random humor.

Grumpy Cat Made a Fortune With One Frown
Her permanently grumpy expression turned her into a meme empire — with books, merchandise, and millions in earnings.

"Chewbacca Mom" Laughed Her Way to Fame
A mom's video of herself laughing hysterically in a Chewbacca mask became one of Facebook's most-viewed clips ever.

"Damn, Daniel" Earned a Lifetime of Vans
Two teens went viral after one kept shouting "Damn, Daniel!" in admiration of his friend's white sneakers — and Vans rewarded them with free shoes for life.

A Potato Went Viral for Doing Nothing
A man streamed himself on Twitch pretending to be a potato for 24 hours. Thousands of people watched. Because, internet.

"Hide the Pain Harold" Is a Real Guy
The man behind the meme is a Hungarian electrical engineer named András Arató — and he's embraced his internet fame with humor and grace.

TikTok Made Corn a Celebrity
A kid who said, "It's corn!" in an interview became an instant meme, landing him on talk shows and even in songs.

A Cat Playing Keyboard Became a Legend
"Keyboard Cat," a video made in the '80s but uploaded decades later, became one of the most iconic memes ever shared.

A Vine of a Lemon Kid Lives Forever
"Lemon kid" and other 6-second Vine classics like "What are those?!" still echo across modern memes — proving short videos have big impact.

The "Dress" That Broke the Internet Was Just About Lighting
Millions argued if a dress was blue and black or white and gold — it turned out to be blue and black, but weird lighting fooled everyone.

A Guy Filming a Skateboard Became a Holiday Icon
Nathan Apodaca went viral after skating to "Dreams" with cranberry juice — even earning a truck and meeting Fleetwood Mac's Mick Fleetwood.

A Banana Taped to a Wall Sold for $120,000
A real banana duct-taped to a wall as "art" went viral — proving that internet fame can turn anything into gold.

"Baby Shark" Is the Most-Watched Video Ever
This children's song became a global earworm, earning over 14 billion views and even charting on Billboard.

A Kid's "Apparently" Speech Made Him TV Famous
Noah Ritter, the "Apparently Kid," went viral after giving an adorably honest interview — and became a talk-show regular.

"Disaster Girl" Made a Fortune From Her Meme
The girl smiling in front of a burning house turned her meme into an NFT, selling it for almost half a million dollars.

A Man With a Skateboard Became an Olympic Coach
Tony Hawk, once just a kid making skateboard videos, became a legend — and helped make skateboarding an Olympic sport.

From dancing babies to viral eggs, the internet has created legends out of pure randomness. It's proof that in the digital age, *anyone* — or anything — can go viral overnight.

The Ice Bucket Challenge Raised $220 Million.

Chapter 36: American Politics & Presidents

U.S. politics might sound serious, but history is packed with bizarre, funny, and unexpected moments from the White House. From pet alligators to pillow fights, presidents have been involved in some truly unforgettable stories. These facts show the human (and often hilarious) side of American leaders.

George Washington Never Lived in the White House
Although he was the first U.S. president, Washington never lived there — the White House wasn't finished until after he died.

John Quincy Adams Enjoyed Skinny Dipping in the Potomac River
Every morning, he went for a swim — completely naked. A female journalist once waited on the shore to interview him until he came out.

Abraham Lincoln Was a Licensed Bartender
Before becoming president, Lincoln co-owned a tavern in Illinois called Berry and Lincoln. He's the only president to hold a bartender's license.

Teddy Roosevelt Had a Pet Alligator at the White House
Roosevelt's kids loved collecting wild animals — including an alligator that occasionally roamed the White House halls.

William Taft Got Stuck in the Bathtub
Taft, who weighed over 300 pounds, once got stuck in a White House bathtub and needed several men to pull him out.

John F. Kennedy Could Read at 1,500 Words Per Minute
JFK was known for speed reading — more than ten times faster than the average reader.

Thomas Jefferson Invented the Swivel Chair
While drafting the Declaration of Independence, Jefferson sat on the first-ever swivel chair — which he designed himself.

Herbert Hoover's Son Had Two Pet Alligators Too
They were allowed to roam the White House grounds and even the bathrooms. Clearly, early presidents had a thing for reptiles.

Richard Nixon Loved Bowling So Much He Built a Private Alley
He had a single-lane bowling alley installed beneath the White House so he could play anytime.

Franklin D. Roosevelt's Dog Caused an International Incident
When critics said he left his dog, Fala, behind on a trip to Alaska, FDR jokingly claimed he'd never "abandon his little dog," turning it into a political win.

Barack Obama Collected Spider-Man Comics
Obama grew up loving Marvel heroes — and later appeared on a special edition Spider-Man comic cover himself.

Grover Cleveland Was the Only President to Serve Two Non-Consecutive Terms
He was both the 22nd and 24th president — technically making him two presidents in one.

Jimmy Carter Saw a UFO
In 1969, before becoming president, Carter reported seeing a glowing object in the sky that he couldn't explain.

Ronald Reagan Was a Lifeguard Who Saved 77 People
Before Hollywood or politics, Reagan worked as a teenage lifeguard and rescued dozens of swimmers.

Lyndon B. Johnson Gave Interviews From His Bathroom
He was known for multitasking — even continuing conversations with reporters while using the toilet.

Bill Clinton Played the Saxophone on Live TV
During his 1992 campaign, Clinton played "Heartbreak Hotel" on *The Arsenio Hall Show*, helping him connect with younger voters.

George H.W. Bush Banned Broccoli from Air Force One
He openly admitted he hated broccoli — and banned it from the presidential plane and White House menu.

Donald Trump Is in the WWE Hall of Fame
He's the only U.S. president officially recognized by World Wrestling Entertainment for his appearances in the ring.

Joe Biden Loves Ice Cream So Much It's a Running Joke
Biden's well-known obsession with ice cream has inspired memes, interviews, and even an official campaign video.

James Madison Was the Shortest President Ever
Standing at just 5'4" and weighing about 100 pounds, Madison was physically small — but played a huge role in writing the Constitution.

Andrew Jackson's Parrot Swore at His Funeral
Jackson's pet parrot had learned so many curse words that it had to be removed from the service for being too loud.

Calvin Coolidge Pressed a Button to Get Rid of Guests
Coolidge had a buzzer under his desk to signal his secretary to "end" boring meetings by pretending he was needed elsewhere.

Ulysses S. Grant Got a Speeding Ticket on a Horse
Even before cars existed, Grant was fined $20 for riding his horse too fast through Washington, D.C.

Benjamin Harrison Was the First President to Have Electricity — But He Was Afraid of It
He refused to touch the light switches in the White House, worried he'd get shocked.

Teddy Roosevelt Was Shot During a Speech — and Kept Talking
He continued speaking for 84 minutes after being shot in the chest, saying, "It takes more than that to kill a Bull Moose."

George W. Bush Once Choked on a Pretzel Watching Football
During his presidency, Bush fainted after choking on a pretzel — and later joked about it in interviews.

Obama Brewed Beer in the White House
He introduced the first-ever homebrewed beer to the White House kitchen — complete with honey from Michelle Obama's garden.

A Cat Once Ran for Mayor in Alaska — and Won
While not a president, "Mayor Stubbs," a cat in Talkeetna, Alaska, served as an honorary mayor for 20 years.

The White House Has a Secret Bunker and a Bowling Alley
Underneath the famous building, there's an underground shelter, a movie theater, and even a chocolate shop.

Behind every polished speech and serious decision, there's a human — sometimes funny, sometimes strange, always fascinating. Politics might shape nations, but these stories remind us that presidents are people too.

Herbert Hoover's Son Had Two Pet Alligators Too.

Lightning Was Once Blamed on Angry Gods.

Chapter 37: Science vs. Beliefs

Throughout history, people have believed in wild ideas — from the Earth being flat to diseases caused by "bad air." But brave scientists kept asking questions, running experiments, and proving what was really true. This chapter dives into those moments when science went head-to-head with superstition — and won.

People Once Thought the Earth Was the Center of the Universe
For centuries, everyone believed the sun revolved around Earth. Copernicus and Galileo proved the opposite — and were criticized for it!

Lightning Was Once Blamed on Angry Gods
Before Benjamin Franklin's kite experiment, people thought lightning was a punishment from the heavens. His discovery of electricity changed that forever.

Witches Were Just Misunderstood Scientists
In the Middle Ages, women using herbs for healing were often accused of witchcraft — but many of their remedies worked and inspired modern medicine.

People Thought the Heart Controlled Emotions
Ancient doctors believed feelings came from the heart, not the brain. Now we know your brain is the real boss of emotions.

The First Surgeon to Use Clean Tools Was Laughed At
In the 1800s, Joseph Lister suggested cleaning instruments to stop infections. Other doctors mocked him — until his patients stopped dying.

People Believed Flies Magically Created Themselves
It took a scientist named Francesco Redi to prove that flies come from other flies — not from rotten meat!

Galileo Was Arrested for Saying Earth Moves
When he used a telescope to prove that planets orbit the sun, the Church called him a heretic. He spent years under house arrest for being right too soon.

Doctors Once Thought "Bad Air" Caused Disease
Before germ theory, people blamed "miasma" or smelly air for sickness. It wasn't until Louis Pasteur proved bacteria were real that modern medicine began.

People Used to Believe in Spontaneous Human Combustion
For years, stories claimed people just burst into flames for no reason. Science later showed it's caused by external heat and body fat acting like candle wax.

Bloodletting Was a Common Cure — For Everything
Doctors used to "bleed" patients to balance their body's "humors." It often made people worse — not better.

The First Vaccination Came From Cowpox
In 1796, Edward Jenner discovered that milkmaids who got cowpox didn't catch smallpox. His idea launched modern immunization.

People Once Thought Tomatoes Were Poisonous
In the 1700s, Europeans avoided tomatoes because they looked like deadly nightshade plants. Now they're on every pizza!

Einstein's Theories Were Once Mocked
When Albert Einstein first published his theory of relativity, many scientists thought it was nonsense — until his predictions were proven right.

Sailors Believed Sea Monsters Caused Storms
For centuries, sailors told tales of giant creatures sinking ships. Science later showed it was rogue waves — not monsters — doing the damage.

People Thought Radio Waves Were Magic
When Guglielmo Marconi sent messages through the air in 1895, many thought it was witchcraft. Now, we call it Wi-Fi.

Doctors Once Smoked in Hospitals
In the 1950s, even doctors didn't know cigarettes were dangerous. It took decades of research to prove the link to cancer.

Meteorites Were Called "Heaven Rocks"
When rocks fell from the sky, people thought they were divine gifts. Scientists later proved they were pieces of asteroids.

The Earthquake Fish Myth
Before seismology, people in Japan believed a giant catfish named Namazu caused earthquakes. Today, scientists use sensors — not superstition — to predict tremors.

People Laughed at the Idea of Germs
When early scientists claimed invisible "germs" caused disease, most doctors refused to believe it. Now, we wash our hands because of them.

Astronomers Once Thought the Moon Was Perfect
They believed it was a flawless heavenly body — until telescopes revealed craters, dust, and shadows.

The First Scientist Who Said "Dinosaurs Existed" Was Mocked
When fossils were found, people thought they belonged to dragons. Scientists later realized they were from ancient reptiles — dinosaurs.

People Thought Earthquakes Were Caused by Underground Winds
Before plate tectonics, scientists believed trapped air made the ground shake. Now we know it's moving crust plates.

Science Proved the Earth Isn't Flat — Again and Again
Even though ancient Greeks already knew it, modern flat-Earth believers keep trying to deny centuries of proof.

Rainbows Were Once Seen as Magic
Before physics explained light refraction, people thought rainbows were signs from the gods. Now we know — it's all sunlight and water droplets.

Microscopes Made the Invisible Visible
When Antonie van Leeuwenhoek looked through his microscope, he discovered an entire world of tiny creatures no one knew existed.

People Once Thought the Brain Was Just "Cooling Fluid"
Early scientists believed the brain's only purpose was to cool blood. Now we know it controls every thought, feeling, and action.

The First X-Ray Was an Accident
Wilhelm Röntgen was experimenting with light when he accidentally discovered X-rays — proving bones could be photographed.

Volcanoes Were Once Thought to Be Angry Gods
Before geology, people believed eruptions were divine punishment. Now we understand magma pressure and tectonic activity cause them.

Science Showed That Fear Can Be Measured
Scientists have mapped brain reactions that trigger fear — proving it's not just "in your head," but a real chemical response.

For centuries, science has battled myths — and changed the world by doing so. These discoveries remind us that questioning what "everyone believes" is how progress begins.

Chapter 38: Unexplained Places & Phenomena

Some places on Earth seem to break all the rules of science. From glowing beaches to humming deserts, the world is filled with mysteries that still puzzle experts today. These are the strange corners of our planet where nature — and maybe something more — refuses to explain itself.

The Bermuda Triangle Still Baffles Scientists
Planes and ships have vanished without explanation in the area between Florida, Bermuda, and Puerto Rico. Some say it's magnetic fields — others, just coincidence.

A Lake in Tanzania Turns Animals Into Stone
Lake Natron's water is so alkaline that it preserves dead animals like statues. It's real-life petrification — not magic.

The Ocean Glows in the Dark
In places like the Maldives, glowing "bioluminescent plankton" make the waves sparkle blue at night. It looks like stars floating in the water.

The "Sailing Stones" Move by Themselves
In Death Valley, huge rocks slide across the desert floor, leaving trails behind. Scientists discovered thin ice sheets and wind are behind the movement.

There's a Place Where Birds Fly in Circles and Fall
In India's Jatinga village, birds crash to the ground at night every year. Scientists blame weather patterns and disorientation — locals once blamed spirits.

The Devil's Kettle Swallows Water — and Nobody Knows Where It Goes
This Minnesota waterfall splits into two. One side flows normally; the other disappears into a hole no one's been able to trace.

The Taos Hum Keeps People Awake
Residents of Taos, New Mexico, report hearing a low hum with no source. Sound experts still can't fully explain it.

Lights Flicker Over the Marfa Desert
In Texas, glowing orbs appear on the horizon — moving, splitting, and vanishing. Scientists think it's refraction, but no one's proven it.

A Giant Eye Appeared in the Sahara
The "Eye of the Sahara" is a massive circular formation visible from space. It's 25 miles wide — and scientists still debate how it formed.

Antarctica Has a "Blood Falls"
A waterfall of red liquid flows from the Taylor Glacier. It's not blood — it's iron-rich water that turns red when exposed to oxygen.

The Door to Hell Has Been Burning for 50 Years
In Turkmenistan, a gas crater accidentally set on fire in 1971 — and it's still burning today.

A Forest in Japan Is Known for Its Silence
Aokigahara, also called the "Sea of Trees," absorbs sound in an eerie way. The dense trees make it almost completely silent.

There's a River That Boils Itself
Deep in the Peruvian Amazon, the "Boiling River" reaches nearly 200°F. No volcano nearby — just superheated underground water.

A Desert in Chile Hasn't Seen Rain in Centuries
The Atacama Desert is the driest place on Earth. NASA even tests Mars rovers there because it's so lifeless.

The Mystery of the Wow! Signal
In 1977, a telescope picked up a 72-second radio signal from space — perfectly structured, never repeated, never explained.

The Stone Spheres of Costa Rica Are Too Perfect
Hundreds of ancient stone spheres are scattered across Costa Rica. Nobody knows who made them or why.

Underwater City Found in Japan
Off Yonaguni Island, divers discovered massive stone structures that look manmade — but no one agrees if it's natural or built.

Trees That "Walk" in the Amazon
Some palm trees slowly move several feet each year as new roots grow toward sunlight — earning the nickname "walking palms."

Water That Flows Backward in Oregon
At Oregon's "Magnetic Hill," cars and water seem to roll uphill. It's actually an optical illusion caused by the landscape.

Mysterious Circles in the Namib Desert
Perfectly round patches of barren earth dot the desert. Some blame termites; others, plants fighting for water.

Fish Rain From the Sky in Honduras
Once or twice a year, small fish literally fall from the sky during storms in a town called Yoro. Scientists think tornadoes suck them from rivers.

There's a Cave That Sings
In New Mexico's Carlsbad Caverns, air flowing through tunnels creates eerie humming and whistling sounds.

Pink Lakes Exist Around the World
Lakes in Australia and Senegal naturally turn pink due to salt-loving algae. They're safe — and totally Instagram-worthy.

Stonehenge Still Keeps Its Secrets
Built thousands of years ago, no one knows exactly how or why the giant stones of Stonehenge were arranged so precisely.

A Place Where Compass Needles Spin Wildly
At Magnetic Hill in Canada, the magnetic pull confuses compasses — cars appear to roll uphill on their own.

A City That Vanished Under the Sea
Off India's coast, ancient ruins were found underwater near Dwarka — matching stories from Hindu texts about a sunken kingdom.

There's a Mountain That Constantly Hums
Mount Taishan in China emits deep, echoing sounds. Scientists suspect underground movement, but locals call it "the mountain's voice."

A Glowing Cave in New Zealand Is Lit by Worms
The Waitomo Caves glow blue at night thanks to bioluminescent worms dangling silk threads to catch prey.

From ghost lights to whispering winds, our planet hides countless mysteries science still can't fully solve. Maybe the next great discovery — or explanation — will come from someone just as curious as you.

There's a River That Boils Itself.

Chapter 39: Dumb Decisions with Big Consequences

Sometimes, the biggest disasters start with the smallest bad ideas. History is full of moments when someone said, "What could go wrong?" — and then *everything* did. These funny, shocking, and downright weird blunders prove that even smart people can make legendary mistakes.

A Typo Lost NASA $80 Million
In 1962, NASA's Mariner 1 spacecraft exploded just after launch because of a single missing hyphen in the code. One typo — one lost rocket.

Napoleon Attacked… by Bunnies
During a celebration hunt, Napoleon Bonaparte's staff released thousands of rabbits. But instead of running away, the bunnies charged and overwhelmed his army.

Someone Once Sold Alaska for Pennies
In 1867, Russia sold Alaska to the U.S. for only $7.2 million — about two cents per acre. Today, it's worth over $100 billion in oil alone.

The Titanic Ignored Ice Warnings
Before the ship sank, multiple radio messages warned of icebergs. The operators were too busy sending personal messages to pay attention.

A War Was Fought Over a Pig
In 1859, a British soldier shot an American farmer's pig in the San Juan Islands. Both nations nearly went to war — over bacon.

The Guy Who Invented Segway Drove Off a Cliff
The owner of the Segway company accidentally rode one off a cliff in 2010 while testing it. Talk about irony on wheels.

A Broken Window Started a Huge Fire
In 1993, a house fire in England was caused when sunlight hit a mirror and focused on curtains. One bad mirror angle — total disaster.

They Built a City Below Sea Level — Without a Drain
New Orleans was built below sea level but had no proper drainage system for years. The result? Floods became part of everyday life.

A Metric Mistake Crashed a $125 Million Spacecraft
NASA's Mars Climate Orbiter burned up because one team used metric units and another used imperial. It literally crashed over a math mix-up.

The Trojan Horse Was Basically an Ancient Prank Gone Wrong
The Greeks pretended to gift a giant wooden horse — but it was filled with soldiers. The Trojans accepted it, bringing doom inside their own walls.

Someone Tried to Ban Coffee — and Failed Hard
In the 1600s, King Charles II of England tried to outlaw coffeehouses, thinking they caused rebellion. People ignored him and kept sipping.

The Great Emu War Was Lost — to Emus
In 1932, Australia sent soldiers with machine guns to fight wild emus destroying crops. The birds outran the army and won.

A Guy Tried to Dry Paint with Fire — and Burned Down a Museum
In 1958, a worker at the Museum of Modern Art used a blowtorch to speed up paint drying. He destroyed priceless artworks instead.

A Nuclear Bomb Was Dropped on North Carolina (Almost)
In 1961, a U.S. bomber accidentally dropped two nuclear bombs. Luckily, the safety switch stopped one — the other came *one wire* away from exploding.

They "Lost" the Only Copy of the Moon Landing Tape
NASA accidentally erased the original Apollo 11 moon landing footage while reusing old tapes. What survived are broadcast copies.

Chernobyl's Meltdown Started with a Safety Test
The world's worst nuclear accident began when engineers ran a safety drill that went completely wrong.

A Man Declared War on the Ocean — and Lost His Job
In 1859, Emperor Norton of San Francisco "declared war" on the Pacific Ocean to stop its waves. Locals loved it — but the government didn't.

They Put the Wrong Guy on the Money
In 2010, Chile printed 1.5 million coins misspelling "Chile" as "Chiie." Instead of recalling them, they became collector's items.

A Candy Bar Company Rejected The Beatles
Decca Records famously turned down The Beatles in 1962, saying "guitar music is on the way out." Oops.

Someone Blew Up a Whale — with Dynamite
In 1970 Oregon, officials tried to dispose of a beached whale with explosives. Whale chunks rained from the sky. Cars were destroyed.

A Bank Once Gave Out $10 Million by Mistake
A New Zealand couple's account was accidentally credited millions. They vanished on the run — and were later caught.

The Leaning Tower of Pisa Was a Construction Fail
It started tilting halfway through building because of weak soil. Instead of fixing it, they just… kept going.

Someone Tried to Clean a Painting — and Wiped the Face Off Jesus
In Spain, a woman's "restoration" of a 19th-century fresco turned it into a meme called "Monkey Christ."

A Simple Delay Caused the Great Chicago Fire
A watchman spotted the fire early but decided to double-check before alerting others. That few-minute delay turned it into a city-wide disaster.

A Ship Captain Ignored a Volcano Warning
In 1883, a captain near Krakatoa ignored signs of eruption. Hours later, the explosion killed tens of thousands — and shattered windows 3,000 miles away.

A Typo Changed a Website Forever
Someone forgot to renew "google.com" in 2015, and a man bought it for $12. Google paid him thousands to get it back.

Someone Forgot to Turn Off a Faucet — for 40 Years
In Italy, a broken fountain leaked continuously from the 1930s to the 1970s, wasting millions of gallons of water before anyone fixed it.

A Man Sold His Apple Stock for $800 — Worth Billions Later
Ronald Wayne, Apple's third co-founder, sold his 10% share in 1976. Today, it would be worth over $100 billion.

From exploding whales to billion-dollar regrets, history proves one thing — even small mistakes can echo through time. So double-check your work… especially if it involves rockets, money, or dynamite.

The Trojan Horse Was Basically an Ancient Prank Gone Wrong.

Chapter 40: The Planet's Weirdest Wonders

Earth is home to some of the strangest and most jaw-dropping sights you could ever imagine. From glowing caves and rainbow mountains to bubbling lakes and forests that turn to stone, nature doesn't always play by the rules. These real places prove that our planet is basically one giant science experiment — and we're lucky enough to live on it.

A Lake That Explodes
Lake Nyos in Cameroon once released a massive cloud of carbon dioxide from deep below, suffocating everything nearby. It's one of the strangest — and deadliest — natural events ever recorded.

A Rainbow Mountain Actually Exists
In Peru, Vinicunca (the Rainbow Mountain) has colorful stripes made from layers of minerals like iron, copper, and sulfur. It looks Photoshopped — but it's 100% real.

Trees That Turn to Stone
The Petrified Forest in Arizona is filled with ancient trees that fossilized over 200 million years ago, turning to colorful quartz.

A Desert Covered in Ice Caves
In Iceland, glaciers form sparkling blue ice tunnels so clear they look like frozen glass. Each winter, new ones appear as old ones melt away.

A Cave That Glows Like the Night Sky
The Waitomo Caves in New Zealand are lit by glowworms that dangle sticky threads to catch bugs. The result? A glowing galaxy underground.

A Lake So Pink It Looks Like Cotton Candy
Lake Hillier in Australia is bright pink thanks to algae and bacteria that love salty water. The color doesn't fade — even when you scoop it up!

Waterfalls That Freeze in Midair
In Antarctica, the "Blood Falls" cascade down a glacier in a shocking red color caused by iron-rich water meeting oxygen.

A River That Changes Colors Like a Rainbow
Colombia's Caño Cristales is called the "River of Five Colors." Special plants beneath the surface make it shimmer in red, yellow, green, blue, and black.

Rocks That Make Music
The "Singing Rocks" in Pennsylvania produce bell-like tones when struck. Scientists think their perfect crystal structure helps them "sing."

A Beach That Glows Blue at Night
Maldive shores sparkle in the dark from bioluminescent plankton. It's like the ocean sprinkled itself with fairy dust.

The Ground That Moves Like Jello
In Canada's Spotted Lake, minerals form colorful spots that shift and bubble as temperatures rise. It looks like Earth is breathing.

A Forest That Grows on Water
In Romania, the "Floating Forest" of Lake Cuejdel stands on a natural raft of fallen logs — trees literally float on the surface.

A Lake That's Fuller of Soda Than Water
Tanzania's Lake Natron is so alkaline it can turn animals that fall in into stone-like sculptures. The high pH preserves their bodies in eerie detail.

A Desert with Waves of Stone
Arizona's "The Wave" is a sandstone formation that looks like a frozen rainbow. It formed from millions of years of wind carving through rock.

A Cave of Giant Crystals You Could Walk Through
Mexico's Naica Mine holds selenite crystals so huge they look like frozen beams of light — some are over 30 feet long!

A Valley That Smells Like Rotten Eggs — and Explodes Sometimes
In Italy's Solfatara crater, volcanic gases create a foul stench and random bursts of steam. Locals call it the "Gates of Hell."

An Island That's a Giant Volcano
Santorini, Greece, formed from one massive volcanic explosion. The island's crescent shape shows where the ancient volcano collapsed.

A Waterfall That Falls Up
In Ireland, strong Atlantic winds blow so fiercely that waterfalls are pushed upward — creating an upside-down cascade!

A Mountain That Looks Like a Face
In Canada, a rock formation called the "Sleeping Giant" looks exactly like a man lying down. Local legends say he turned to stone after being betrayed.

A Hill That Defies Gravity
At Magnetic Hill in India, cars appear to roll uphill on their own. It's all an optical illusion — but it's freaky to watch.

A Desert That Blooms Overnight
Every few years, Chile's Atacama Desert bursts into millions of colorful flowers after rare rainfall. It's one of nature's most unexpected surprises.

The World's Tallest Waterfall Hides in a Jungle
Angel Falls in Venezuela drops more than 3,200 feet — so tall that much of the water evaporates before hitting the ground.

A Cave That Breathes
In New Mexico, "Breathing Cave" seems to inhale and exhale air as temperatures shift. The airflow is caused by underground pressure changes.

A Beach That "Barks" When You Step On It
Japan's Naki Suna Beach makes squeaky "barking" sounds as sand grains rub together. Tourists call it the "singing sand beach."

A Valley That Hums Like a Giant Speaker
California's Death Valley sometimes produces a deep, mysterious humming sound caused by sand avalanches vibrating in unison.

The Ocean Has a Waterfall Underwater
Near Mauritius, sand from the ocean floor slides off a shelf, creating the illusion of a giant underwater waterfall.

A Lake That's So Clear It's Like Glass
In New Zealand, Blue Lake has the clearest natural water on Earth — visibility reaches 250 feet deep!

From pink lakes to glowing caves, Earth never runs out of surprises. Our planet is the ultimate artist — creating beauty that's weird, wild, and completely real.

A Cave of Giant Crystals You Could Walk Through.

Chapter 41: The Celts
– Warriors, Wizards, and Ancient Mysteries

Before castles, knights, and kings — there were the Celts!
These fearless tribes ruled parts of Europe thousands of years ago, leaving behind stories of magic, battles, and breathtaking art.
They didn't write much down, but their legends still shape our fantasy worlds today.

The Celts once lived across most of Europe — from Spain to Turkey, forming hundreds of tribes connected by language, art, and beliefs.

They spoke dozens of languages — but only a few Celtic ones survive today, like Irish Gaelic, Welsh, and Breton.

Celtic warriors dyed their hair bright blue before battle — using a plant called *woad* to look fierce and otherworldly.

They fought completely naked to intimidate enemies — and according to Roman writers... it actually worked!

The word "Celtic" comes from the Greek word *Keltoi* — meaning "the hidden people."

They believed oak trees were sacred — symbols of strength and a link between the earth and the sky.

Druids were more than priests — they were philosophers, healers, judges, and astronomers all in one.

The Celts celebrated New Year's on Samhain — the ancient festival that later became Halloween.

Celtic knots have no beginning or end — representing eternity, unity, and the endless cycle of life.

Music was at the heart of Celtic life — they played harps, flutes, and drums during every ritual and feast.

They believed in "thin places" — mystical spots where the real world meets the spirit world.

Celtic art hid secret meanings — spirals, circles, and animal shapes symbolized power, growth, and nature.

Women could be warriors and rulers — the legendary Queen Boudicca led an entire army against the Romans.

The Celts mastered ironworking early — crafting strong weapons long before many other ancient cultures.

They brewed beer and mead thousands of years ago — even before the Vikings appeared in history.

Their fashion was colorful and bold — wool cloaks fastened with bronze pins instead of buttons.
The Celts loved storytelling — their bards were like ancient celebrities, honored for keeping legends alive.
Many modern names have Celtic roots — including Arthur, Fiona, and Brian.
Celtic mythology inspired modern fantasy — from *The Lord of the Rings* to *Harry Potter*.
No one knows exactly why the Celts disappeared — their culture merged with others, but their spirit still lives on.

From blue-haired warriors to druidic wisdom, the Celts left behind a world of mystery and magic that still inspires us today.

Celtic warriors dyed their hair bright blue before battle.

The End — Or Just the Beginning?

Wow — you made it! You've just explored some of the wildest, weirdest, and most fascinating truths our world has to offer. From glowing oceans and lost cities to billion-dollar mistakes and mind-blowing inventions, you've seen how strange, funny, and endlessly surprising reality can be. But here's the best part — curiosity never really ends. Every question you ask, every mystery you chase, and every "wait, is that *true?*" moment opens the door to something new. The world is full of stories waiting to be discovered — maybe the next one will be yours.
So keep wondering. Keep asking. Keep exploring.
Because the more you learn, the more amazing the world becomes.

**Would you like to become our book tester?
Don't wait – grab your free copies now!
Give us your email:**

Printed in Dunstable, United Kingdom

74457488R00077